Life of the Moselle,
FROM ITS SOURCE IN THE VOSGES MOUNTAINS TO ITS JUNCTION WITH THE RHINE AT COBLENCE
BY
OCTAVIUS ROOKE

PREFACE.

The beautiful scenery of the Moselle has too long been left without notice. It is true, some of our Artists have presented to us scenes on the banks of this river; but English travellers are, for the most part, ignorant how very charming and eminently picturesque are the shores of this lovely stream.

"The Rhine! the Rhine!" is quoted by every one, and admired or abused at every fireside, but the Moselle is almost wholly unexplored. Lying, as she does, within a district absolutely overrun with summer-tourists, it is altogether inexplicable that a river presenting scenery unsurpassed in Europe should be so neglected by those who in thousands pass the mouth of her stream. When the Roman Poet Ausonius visited Germany, it was not the Rhine, but the Moselle which most pleased him; and although glorious Italy was his home, yet he could spare time to explore the Moselle, and extol the loveliness of her waters in a most eloquent poem.[x]

The Moselle, which rises among the wooded mountains of the Department des Vosges, never during its whole course is otherwise than beautiful. Below Trèves it passes between the Eifel and Hunsruck ranges of mountains, which attain to the height of ten or twelve hundred feet above the level of the river.

In the Thirty Years' War the Moselle country suffered severely from the ravages of the different armies; but there still remain on the shores of this river more old castles and ruins, and more curious old houses, than can elsewhere be found in a like space in Europe.

Having in the following pages endeavoured to lay before English readers the interesting scenery of the Moselle, I trust, that although in summer my countrymen do not mount her stream, fearful, perhaps, of discomfort; yet that by the fireside in winter the public will not object to glide down the river, in the boat now ready for them to embark in; and hoping that they will enjoy the reproduction of a tour that afforded me so much pleasure,

I subscribe myself

Their humble servant,

THE AUTHOR.

Richmond, December 1857.[xi]

Source.

At a short distance from Bussang, a little town in the Department des Vosges in France, is the source of the Moselle; trickling through the moss and stones that, together with fallen leaves, strew the ground, come the first few drops of this beautiful river.

A few yards lower down the hill-side, these drops are received into a little pool of fairy dimensions; this tiny pool of fresh sweet water is surrounded by mossy stones, wild garlic, ferns, little creepers of many forms, and stems of trees.

The trees, principally pine, grow thickly over the whole ballon (as the hills are here called); many are of great size; they shut out the heat of the sun, and clothe the earth with tremulous shadows—tremulous, because the broad but feathery ferns receive bright rays, and waving to and fro in the gentle breeze give the shadows an appearance of constant movement.

Here, then, O reader, let us pause and contemplate the birth-place of our stream; leaving the world of stern reality, let us plunge together into the grateful spring of sweet romance; and while the only sounds of life that reach our ears are the rustling of the leaves, the buzz of the great flies, the murmur of the Moselle, and the distant ringing of the woodman's axe, let us return with Memory into the past, and leaving even her behind, go back to those legendary days when spirits purer than ourselves lived and gloried in that beautifully created world which we are daily rendering all unfit for even the ideal habitation of such spirits.

And reverie is not idleness; in hours like these we seem to see before us, cleared from the mists of daily cares, the better path through life—the broad straight path, not thorny and difficult, as men are too prone to [3]paint it, but strewed with those flowers and shaded with those trees given by a beneficent Creator to be enjoyed rightly by us earthly pilgrims.

Life is a pilgrimage indeed, but not a joyless one. While the whole earth and sky teem with glory and beauty, are we to believe that these things may not be enjoyed? Our conscience answers, No; rightly to enjoy, and rightly to perform our duties, with thankfulness, and praise, and love within our hearts, such is our part to perform, and such the lesson we are taught by the fairy of the sweet Moselle.

BIRTH OF THE MOSELLE.

The fair Colline slept in sunshine, when from the far horizon a rain-cloud saw her beauty, and with impetuous ardour rushing through the sky he sought the gentle Colline, wooed her with soft showers, and decked her with jewelled drops and bright fresh flowers.

She soon learnt to love the rugged cloud, and from their union sprang a bright streamlet which, cradled in its mother's lap, reflected her sweet image. Then, as the time passed on, the little one increased in strength, and leapt and danced about its mother's knee. Larger and stronger grew the streamlet until its tripping step became more firm, and then it passed into the valley, catching reflections from the things around. And onward went this fairy stream, her source watched over by a mother's love; and her cloud-father fed her as she passed between her grassy banks.[4]

Then girlhood came, and sister streams flowed in, and, whispering to her, told their little tales of life: so now, her mind enlarged, she onward flows, sometimes reflecting on the things of earth, but oftener expanding her pure bosom to catch the impress of the holy sky; and all the tenants of the sky loved to impart their infinite beauties and their glory to the pure stream.

The age of girlhood passes now away, and she becomes a fair maiden, to gaze on whose beauties towers and cities, castles, spires, and hills, come crowding, and line her path, each giving her the gift of its own being.

Now come the mountains, too, with their crowns of forest waving on their heads, and do homage to her beauty: [5]she gives a sweet smile to all, lingering at every turn to look back upon her friends; but yet she tarries not, her duty leads her on,—nor worldly pomp, or pride, or power, can keep her from her appointed path; she leaves them all behind, and swelling onwards through the level plain, receives the approving glance of heaven, and meets her noble husband Rhine, who, long expecting, folds her in his arms. And thus her pilgrimage complete, her duty ended, she calmly sleeps that happy sleep which wakes only in eternity.

Such is the history of the birth and life of the Moselle. We have now to wander from her birthplace here, in the Vosges mountains, to where she joins her glorious husband Rhine beneath the walls of Ehrenbreitstein. From time to time we shall linger by the roadside, to pluck a flower from legendary lore; from time to time we shall stop to secure a chip from the great rock of history: storing thus our herbal and our sack as well as our portfolio, we shall follow the many bendings of our graceful river, which, womanlike, moves gently and caressingly along, soothing and gladdening all things.

The fairy and the river are as one, life within life; ever flowing on, yet always present; ever young, and yet how old; ever springing freshly mid the hills and woods, yet ever ending the appointed course.

One life is material, earthly, but still sweet and beautiful; the other life is born of the first, but far exceeds [6]it,—it is the life poetic, whose other parent is the human mind: this life, which leaves the parent life behind, floats upwards on its glorious wings and reaches the highest realms of heaven, carrying with it the souls of those who read this life aright——

Lying here beneath the pines, we recall those old days of the past when, on the borders of our river, only forests waved, amid whose depths tribes of wild warriors dwelt apart,—their only amusement hunting, their only business war, they scorned to cultivate the soil save for their actual necessities.

In this neighbourhood lived the Leuci, whose capital was Toul; lower down, the Mediomatrices had their chief city, Metz; and beyond these again came the Treviri, occupying the country about Trèves.

All these were members of that great German family which gave sea-kings to Norway, conquerors to imperial Rome, and at a later day that champion (Charles Martel) who stayed the tide of Moslem conquest near Poitiers; thus Christianising half Europe, and probably saving all earth from Mahomet's false creed.

Rugged and strong were these old Germans—the huge pines well represent them; glorious in strength, stern in duty, upright, sombre, and picturesquely magnificent: they are recorded as having been of great size, with blue eyes and light hair, inured to every hardship, and never laying aside their arms.[2]

Owning no superior, yet when once they had elected a chief, and raised him aloft upon their shields, they obeyed him implicitly; if unsuccessful in battle they would kill themselves rather than survive, believing that those who died on the battle-field were received by the Walkyren, or heavenly maidens, who hovered over the fight and chose lovers from the dying warriors.

What a picture of barbaric grandeur and indomitable will is given us in the last act of one of their more northern naval heroes! Being mortally wounded in a fight in which he had conquered his enemies, he caused himself to be placed on board his vessel with the bodies of his slain enemies around him, and all his plunder piled into a throne, on which he sat,— then the sails were set, the pile was lighted, and the blazing vessel putting out to sea, he sought his heaven—Walhalla.

This Walhalla was supposed to contain a great battle-field, on which the warriors fought their foes all day, receiving no hurt; and at evening they returned to carouse and enjoy the caresses of the Walkyren.

Of these immediate tribes, however, Cæsar relates, that "they only worshipped the forms of the gods they could see and whose beneficence they felt, such as the sun, moon, and fire; of others they had never heard." Doubtless, in after days, they adopted many of the Roman divinities, but at the time of which we speak they adored their Creator on the mountain tops; and when Christianity was introduced they built their churches on the tops of hills, and even now the sacred [8]edifices are usually placed on eminences. Some remnant of the old hill-worship still remains, for the Mass is annually read to the Sens shepherds on the Alps; and not long ago the Saint John's fire was yearly lit upon the hill-tops.

Christmas was their most holy time; for then, they said, the gods walked on earth.

The oak and the alder were objects of especial reverence; for from the former man was made, and woman from the latter.

They considered all trees, and flowers, and plants, and stones, and even animals, to be inhabited by beings of a superior order, who came from an intermediate heaven and hell.

Lakes, rivers, and springs, were held in special veneration; and Petrarch relates, that even in the fourteenth century the women at Cologne bathed in the Rhine to wash away their sins.

Strangely in their natures were intermixed the gentle and the savage, the cruel and the terrible, with the honourable and brave. Side by side we find human sacrifices and a festival in honour of the first violet; men who had been mutilated, and sickly children were sunk in morasses, or otherwise destroyed; and we find them with a pure love for woman, whom they held in the highest reverence. Their women were brought up in the strictest seclusion, scarcely seeing any stranger,—an injury offered to female modesty was punished by death, and fines for injuries done to them were heavier than for those to men.[9]

Maidens were portionless, so only married for their merits or their beauty: they seldom married before their twentieth year, and the husband had generally reached his thirtieth; they had but one husband, and the historian Tacitus observes, speaking of them, "as she can have but one body and one life, so she can have but one husband."

Prophetesses were frequent, and great confidence placed in their predictions,—they were called Alrunæ, and lived apart in the recesses of the forests.

They had many ways of interpreting the will of the gods, but of all interpreters the horse was considered the most sacred; white horses were peculiarly venerated, and

3

maintained at the expense of the community, expressly to interpret the divine will,—even the priests themselves considered that they were but the ministers, while the horses were the confidants of the gods.

The priests, as in all semi-barbarous countries, were the real governors of these uncurbed Germans: no control but theirs was submitted to; even in camp they alone had the right to bind and flog, and in all public assemblies they kept order: these functions they assumed as ministers of the supreme, invisible Being. There was, however, no priestly *caste*, and each head of a family could perform religious offices for his own household.

Thus we find, at this earliest period of the known history of our river—its banks occupied by a brave, hardy race, given to dissipation and war, and governed by priests whose bloody sacrifices were offered to a [10]supreme Being, worshipped through His great emblems of sun, fire, and water—they enjoyed a life of action, and looked forward to a death of glory.

Under this rugged nature appear the gentler attributes of love and veneration; and a belief in Fairies, Kobolds, Nixies, and all the different classes of superior existences with which they supposed the whole world to teem.

Savage and grand, loving and honourable, we shall, if we examine history, find them first engaging the Romans on equal terms, then for a while giving place to the conquerors of the world, but ever holding themselves superior to them, not adopting their habits but merely borrowing their knowledge to render themselves more fit to encounter them; and finally, we shall find them supplanting these world-conquerors, and seizing for themselves that crown and dominion, the fairest portion of which remains with the German race to this present day. And, moreover, it is this German race that has carried civilisation over the whole earth, and whose descendants, the English people, are rapidly populating the great continents of America and Australia.

Back from the train of old history our thoughts return as the evening closes in by the source of our sweet river, and we bend our steps down through the dim woods. The white butterflies flap past, heavily, as though feeling the last moments of their short lives are fleeting fast; frequently above our heads starts out a projecting mass of rock, from whose summit a great [11]pine towers up, first leaning forward, then shooting upwards, its top seems piercing the blue sky.

Ever and anon open out green dells, filled with bright foxgloves and other beautiful flowers; through these dells trickle tiny rivulets that swell the course of our young stream, which through the woods we hear gurgling and gushing on, falling from stone to stone, and wearing many a little pool in the rough ground.

Occasionally we pass a heap of fresh-cut wood, and across our path lie huge trunks of the fallen forest giants; a resinous odour is strongly mixed with the scent of the wild flowers,—one flower, from which the mountain bees make their delicious honey, is peculiarly fragrant and very frequent; occasionally the rivulet is quite hid by the luxuriant carpets of the false forget-me-not that line its banks.

At length we pass from the forest to the cultivated land: the little valley opens into a wider one, which is surrounded by mountains of diverse forms steeped in sunlight; the sun declines, and wreaths of blue smoke ascend from the châlets on the hill-sides, where the evening meal is being prepared for the active, hard-working peasantry, who, with loads of all sorts on their heads, pass by, saluting politely as they go us and each other.

The young stream dances along by the roadside, and thus we enter Bussang, and close our first chapter of this fairy life.[12]

[Contents]

CHAPTER II.

Confluence.

From Bussang to Remiremont our infant stream gurgles plashingly along; sometimes it conceals itself in little tranquil pools, where the large trout lie deep beneath the roots of the overshadowing trees; sometimes it falls with a gentle splash over an obstruction, leaping, as we do in early life, over all difficulties with a smile, even seeming to enjoy that which at a maturer age too often frets and chafes us, though we conceal our chagrin under an unruffled surface.

Sometimes our stream passes, broken into ripples, [13]over smooth shiny pebbles,—here the trout from time to time suddenly dart up and seize their insect food; and sometimes it glides between green banks which hem it in (fair setting for so bright a gem): here it is blue, reflecting the sky above.

Through the sultry summer days, hours spent splashing in this little stream, or dreaming on its banks, are most delicious,—but beware, O bather! of the shining pebbles that gleam mid the blue tide, for

> Beneath the waters bright
> The glitt'ring pebbles lie,
> Like nymphs whose eyes the light
> Shines on with brilliancy:
> Like wicked water-sprites
> These rounded pebbles trip
> The bather, who delights
> His body here to dip.
> The timid foot is placed
> Upon the tempting stone,
> Then downward in all haste
> The luckless wight is thrown.
> And when he wrathful tries
> His footing to regain,
> The sprites, with shining eyes,
> Just trip him up again.

The scenery down the valley is altogether charming, occasionally grand, but oftener sweetly beautiful; the hills are of considerable height, some cultivated in patches of grain-crops, some covered with trees, while others again are brightly green with turf, except where [14]grey rocks crop out and break the outline. Farther off the large shadowy mountains rise, calmly shutting in the minor hills, the valley, and the stream; the fleecy clouds float gently on, and rest upon their summits.

Groups of trees half hide the houses which frequently appear within the valley; the numerous bridges are generally of wood, some covered as in Switzerland.

The peasant women, in great straw hats or little close caps, work hard amidst the fields storing the hay crop; the oxen yoked together munch their fill of sweet fresh grass, that has grown in the well-watered meadows; round them the children play, piling the hay upon each other until, overcome by the heat, they hasten off to bathe in our cool stream.

Here, at a short distance above Remiremont, is the confluence of two branches of our river; and river the Moselle now becomes. Leaving her infant days she glides forth, with all the sunny joyousness of girlhood, through the valleys of Remiremont and Épinal, then on through the undulating plain, past Toul, to meet her confidant the Meurthe.

Remiremont is a well-built, clean town, with rivulets flowing constantly on both sides the roadway; it contains a fine church, near which are the buildings that formerly held the celebrated Dames de Remiremont, of whom the following account is given.

In the seventh century a monk named Amé arrived at the court of King Theodobert of Austrasia; moved [15]by his preaching, one of the principal officers of the king, named Romaric, embraced the monastic life, and gave an estate to found a monastery of nuns: the mountain on which this monastery was built was called "Mons Romarici," hence the modern name of Remiremont.

A community of monks was established shortly after, near the nunnery, and St. Amé governed both; he dying, Romaric succeeded him: but now the female monastery was governed by an abbess,—it is said, a daughter of Romaric.

To this monastery Charlemagne came to enjoy the pleasures of the chase, and here the unhappy Waldrada, wife of Lothaire II., came to die after her long persecution by the Church.

In the tenth century the Huns penetrated here, and ravaged the monastery; a few years after it was totally destroyed by fire; after this event it was rebuilt at the foot of the mountain: the two communities now separated, the ladies entering on their new abode, and the monks retiring to the mountain.

The ladies lived such scandalous lives that Pope Eugenius reproached them with dishonouring the religious habit; his complaints were useless, and the ladies soon threw off even the appearance of *religieuses*, and remained bound together by a sort of female feudality. The abbesses were people of the best families, and none were admitted as members of the community but those who could prove themselves of noble blood on both sides for two hundred years.[16]

The abbess ranked as a princess of the Empire, and held a feudal court,—a drawn sword was carried before her by one of the officers, of whom she had many in her service; she received her investiture from the hands of the Emperor himself, and had many rights over different parts of the surrounding country, her power often clashing with that of the Dukes of Lorraine.

The Dukes were bound to appear before the monastery on the 15th of July of each year, and to carry on their shoulders the shrine of St. Romaric; they then signed, in a large book plated with gold and kept for that purpose, a confirmation of all the privileges of the abbey. In consideration of these services, however, they gained certain solid advantages.

One of the most violent quarrels between "les Dames" and the Dukes of Lorraine was owing to Duke Charles III. refusing to carry the saint's relics on his shoulders; eventually the ladies gave up the point on consideration of receiving, in lieu, an annuity of 400 francs.

In 1637 Duke Charles IV. besieged the town, which had been garrisoned by the French with fifteen companies of the regiment of Normandy. These soldiers being driven to extremity, declared, rather than submit without conditions, they would burn the abbess, abbey, and all the ladies, as well as the citizens; the ladies despatched six of their number to the Duke, who, overcome by the tears of beauty, granted an advantageous capitulation to the Norman rascals.

Next year Turenne appeared before the city, which [17]the Duke had left feebly garrisoned; but the abbess, mindful of the Duke's kindness, so stoutly defended it, that after three assaults Turenne retired with considerable loss. After this the abbess obtained from the French king a promise of neutrality.

The power of these extraordinary "Dames de Remiremont" lasted (though somewhat shorn) until the tide of the French Revolution swept away for a time even the name of the town, which was called Libremont. The church and buildings still remain, the last remnants of this extraordinary community.

Having climbed the hills above Remiremont and seated ourselves amid the heather and ferns, the valley in folds of bright green extends itself beneath; the hills around are varied and beautiful, clumps of trees adorn the meadows, and great shadows steal along, presenting to our eyes a constant succession of moving pictures.

One of these shadows we watch roll down the distant mountain-side, leaving it bright and glowing with the grain,—then, coming onwards, it rests upon a great clump of trees, whose contrasted darkness lights up the grass beyond: they in their turn are left behind, and, now quivering in light, they stand backed by the sombre mountain wrapped in a succeeding veil; these clouds roll on, and others quickly following, give to the valley an appearance similar to that of a rolling prairie: now they approach, and envelope the hill on which we sit in gloom; but shortly all again is clear, the sky above is pure, the air is sweet; the meadows [18]glory in their abundance, and our river, bending and turning, now to the far side of the valley, now towards the town, freshens the heated herbage with its limpid stream.

From the valley, beautiful though it be, we turn our eyes to the more glorious beauty of the

NOONDAY CLOUDS.
Over our heads the sunbeams quiver,
The air is filled with heat and light,
While at our feet the shining river

6

Sparkles with thousand dimples bright.
The distant hills, in sombre masses,
Sleep calmly on amidst the haze;
A mighty cloud through heaven passes,
And from the earth arrests our gaze.
For in the shadows of that cloud,
We seem to see extending far
Valleys and hills, where seraphs bow'd,
Praising their great Creator are.
Praising for ever "Him on high."
Those glorious seraphs also pray,
That from this planet crime may die,
From man and earth sin pass away.
The shades of these hills of central air,
The gales that spring 'mid their lake,
Spread over our earthly valleys fair,
From our souls the weariness take;
And hope reviving emits its glad beam,
Which brightens our hearts, as sun does the stream.

Where we sit the ground is heaped into all sorts of forms, and covered with ferns and heather,—from the [19]latter rushes a large covey of whirring partridges, and swoops into the valley.

Above, the still forest sends down its treasures of bark and firewood, which are borne in creaking waggons down the steep ascent; the oxen stagger beneath the weight, while the drivers shout encouragement, and their great dogs look calmly from the overhanging bank upon the busy scene.

All the environs of Remiremont are beautiful, and the town itself is a favourable specimen of a French country town: it is much better paved than those towns usually are, and the principal street has arcades under the first floor, beneath whose shade it is pleasant to sit during the midday heat, and hear the water rushing through the tiny canals.

In the little busy inns people come and go rapidly, the fashionable watering-place of Plombières being only some twelve miles distant: the tables d'hôte at these inns are wonderful, the number of dishes, the rapidity with which they are served, and the really excellent cookery. Most of the diners are men, and they one and all make love to the woman who, in conjunction with a lad, waits on some twenty guests, and yet finds time to parry all their jokes with sharp repartee.

Here may be seen a good specimen of the false politeness of the French,—they never help themselves to the *vin ordinaire* without filling up their neighbour's glass, whether he wants more or not, and they almost invariably pick out the choice morsel from the dish which the aforesaid neighbour eyes with longing looks: [20]one, an epicure, reaches over you to secure the oil and pepper, with which to make additions to some vile sauce he is compounding for a coming dish; another *will* have something out of its proper turn, which irritates the handmaid; all eat voraciously, and with knives scoop up superfluous gravy, endangering the fair proportions of their mouths. After dinner (which is at twelve), cards and coffee fill the time until a little gentle exercise brings them to a second dinner at seven, when the knives play their part again.

Travelling in the smaller diligences is very miserable, but the little rattling carts that can be hired are worse and slower. Journeying, again, brings out the *politeness* of the French men,—who secure the best seats if possible, never giving them up to ladies, and fill the vehicle with very bad tobacco smoke.

Leaving them to the smoke and dust, we will go down into the meadows, and walk with our fresh river through the fields it waters on its passage to the gay town of Épinal.

Nurses and Children.

[21]

7

On a slight elevation at the entrance of the town is a public garden of fine old beech-trees, that shade seats and walks; rough grass lawns fill the intervening spaces. Here plays a military band on Sundays and fête-days, and the young men sun themselves in the eyes of the fair ladies, who in many-hued attire float up and down, ostensibly listening to the military music, but really to that of the voices of their admirers.

Here on all days play the children, and on the grass sit the picturesquely-dressed nurses, with great bows in their hair and snowy sleeves puffed out upon their arms. It is a pleasant lounge and of considerable extent; on one side is the river, the main body of which falls over a wear, while a portion of the water is conducted through the town in a clear stream, which reunites itself with the main body below the town: thus an island is formed, and Epinal stands on both banks as well as on this island, several bridges joining the different quarters.

There is near the end of the town a very beautiful old church; on the hill above, was formerly a strong castle, only a few stones of which now remain: the hill is covered by a private garden commanding fine views.

Epinal is on the site of a very ancient town that was twice destroyed by a fire and pillage; the modern town arose round the walls of a monastery founded in 980 A.D. by a Bishop of Metz, and enlarged in the following century.

The ladies of this monastery appear to have rivalled [22] the "Dames de Remiremont" in leading scandalous lives, if not in power; and when, in the thirteenth century, a Bishop of Toul undertook to re-establish the primitive rules among them, they refused to take any vow, and ended by secularising themselves, but still kept in some measure aloof from the world: they had two dresses, one for the convent, the other for society. They existed as a community till last century.

As a Bishop of Metz had founded this monastery, his successors assumed the sovereignty of the town, and one of them, in the thirteenth century, caused it to be fortified. This sovereignty was often disputed by the townspeople on the one hand, and by certain seigneurs, who had been declared guardians of the monastery, on the other: thus many disputes arose; at last it was agreed that the town should be ceded to the Dukes of Lorraine, and to this house it remained attached.

Frequently taken by the French, and as often retaken, it suffered much from war, but was always constant to its ducal rulers until Lorraine became finally incorporated in France. At the present day it is bustling, dirty, thriving, and ill-paved.

And now away, over the hills and valleys. The river swells on beneath or past us, leaving Thaon, Châtel, Charmes, and many other towns and villages behind; on it flows, falling over wears and circling many islands, wearing its course along until it leaves the Department des Vosges and enters on that of the Meurthe.[23]

Laughing and gay, we shall in the next chapter find "the fair girl" basking amid the corn-fields that adorn her course near Toul.

River Fall.

[24]
[Contents]

CHAPTER III.

Bathing at Toul.

"Oh, pleasant land of France!" sings the poet; and a pleasant land it is, especially when, as now, the tall and yellow grain is spreading over its fair plains. As we approach Toul the reapers are at work; the women and children are busy binding or spreading out the sheaves [25] fast as the men can cut them,—all is gay and happy; the sun glowing on the grain makes the whole land seem an El Dorado, and we appear to move in one of the golden dreams of fairyland.

Coming on our river again, which has serpentined along, loitering to water those fruitful plains of "old Lorraine," we find her stream shrunk within its pebbly bed; for the sun has drunk from earth her moisture, and the fire element rules now for the good of man, where the water, moistening the earth, had produced the germ within her bosom.

The contrast of the burning sun and corn makes our dear river seem the cooler and the fresher. All down its course the bathers are wading refreshingly about: in a side-stream, shaded by tall poplars and guarded from eyes inquisitive by rows of piled-up firewood, bathe the women, maids, and girls; in long loose dresses floating, with hair wreathed lightly round their glistening heads, they toss the glittering drops upon each other, and laugh, and scream, and sing: here, hand-in-hand, with tottering gait, they struggle up against the stream, slipping and tumbling at each forward step,—then, the desired point reached, merrily they float down, and the blue tide sparkles with their beauty. Upon the bank are some timidly adventuring their hesitating feet before they plunge into the element; some bind their hair, preparing; others, having bathed, unbind, and the long tresses stream over the fair shoulders: blithely thus they pass the time, and defy the hot old sun upon the river's bank. [26]

A little further, and the green slopes of the fortifications sweep up, and the cathedral towers stand high above the invisible town; beyond the towers is a great flat-topped hill, whose smaller brethren stretch south-wards: in all, the same flatness of the summit is perceptible.

The river makes a great bend after passing Toul; she seems to have come so far, to see the old capital of the Leuci, and finding there little to arrest her progress or detain her steps, she hastens off to hear from her girlish friend, the Meurthe, the history of Nancy, whose walls the latter guards.

Before we go with our Moselle to hear the tales of Nancy, we must first listen to a simple story from French every-day life, near Toul.

[Contents]

ADÈLE AND GUSTAVE.

Once more War stalked the land; again France was arming, and calling on her sons to fight a foreign foe: but this time her quarrel was a righteous one, for side by side with England she appeared, to guard the weak against the oppression of the strong.

Adèle's heart was beating with anxiety when the day for drawing the fatal numbers had arrived,—those numbers that should determine whether Gustave left her for the battle-field or remained to marry, as had been agreed between them and their parents.

Gustave, however, though he dearly loved his sweet *fiancée*, loved more that empty trumpet glory, a grand [27] word, and one that chains the hearts of men,—but, like the drum and trumpet, its appropriate adjuncts, only expressing a hollow though a ringing sound.

Such was the glory Gustave dreamt of,—not true glory, not heroism in daily life, not the dying in defence of what we love,—but the rush and the glitter, the pomp and the pride, the excitement and the turmoil of the imagined war.

Little thought he of the days of severe privation, the nights of watching, the constant petty troubles, and the lingering pains brought on by disease engendered by a soldier's life; and still less, it is to be feared, did his mind dwell on the number of Adèles this ruthless war leaves mourning and trembling, while their husbands, friends, and lovers, fight and die afar. He only thought of glory in the abstract; perhaps also of a time when, a high grade won, triumphant he should return and lay his spoil at Adèle's feet.

And he was drawn; his friends begged him to let them purchase a substitute,—he, with his ambition and his love for them combined, would not allow that they should thus impoverish themselves; but, being strongly urged, he turned to where Adèle silently was grieving, and left the choice to her.

Poor Adèle, knowing well his secret heart, and fearing that he would only fret and chafe at home,—perhaps, too, being herself a little tainted with his love for glory,—wept, but said, "Go, then, dear Gustave; never shall a French girl counsel her lover to desert his country." [28]

So, while many a tear and secret prayer are poured out for his welfare, Gustave goes.

The land rings with martial preparations; on all sides is the excitement of the coming war: the eagles and the banners are raised high; and all the air is filled with the grand anthem, "PARTANT POUR LA SYRIE."

Part II.

Gustave wrote often: first he was learning his drill, then he had finished his initiation and was in favour with his superiors, often being able to assist with his clear head and ready pen.

Soon after these, a letter came to say the regiment was to hasten to Marseilles, there to embark for Eastern service.

A long silence, and a battle had been fought upon the plains of Alma: his name was not in the lists of killed and wounded,—those fearful lists that break the hearts of many; it is not those fighting, but those left behind we ought to pity.

Then came a day of joy: Gustave had performed one of those daring feats of which the Russian war gave so many instances,—he had been promoted; and Adèle's eyes sparkled, and her bosom heaved, as friends came flocking in offering their congratulations.

The long winter was rolling on; still the enemy, with desperate courage, defended the beleaguered city; and men died fast of fatigue, and cold, and want, both within and without the walls.[22]

Gustave was strong and healthy, never sick or suffering; but, alas! a day came when, after a night sortie gallantly repelled by the French, who followed the enemy nearly into the very town, it was found that he had not returned; and his men reported that he had fallen mortally wounded close to the city walls: they had endeavoured to bring him off, but the task was too difficult, and he was left to breathe his last where he had fallen.

The Colonel himself wrote to his friends, and a decoration was forwarded; but did those words of praise, did that cold cross, repay Adèle for her lost lover? Often, when no eye but that of God was on her, she sat with these treasures in her lap, but from her eyes the tears would flow, and the cross and words were dimly seen through the descending drops,—no, Adèle was not consoled, though he had died for France; hollow were to her the words, "MOURIR POUR LA PATRIE."

Part III.

Peace was with the earth again; the dear-bought peace, that found parents and children, wives and sisters, mourning for those the war had snatched from their embrace.

Around the walls of Toul the harvest had been gathered; the last few sheaves were loaded on the carts as the declining sun sank down; the horses or oxen, gaily decked, moved slowly towards the city; round [30] the waggons the children danced, and thus the maidens sang as in the olden time:—

THE HARVEST SONG.
Our labour all is done;
We've finished with the sun,
Who now, in the far west
Low sinking, goes to rest.
The golden grain is stored;
The Great God be adored,
Who sent the sun and rain
To swell the golden grain.
The stalwart oxen strong
Drag the great wain along;
The last ray from the sun
Shines on our work now done.
Twine, then, the garlands gay;
Let, then, the music play;
And gaily dance till morn,
And fill the flowing horn:
For now the grain is stored,
The Great God be adored,
Who sent the sun and rain
To swell the golden grain.

Adèle entered not into their joy, her heart was like her lover—dead. As they go with the last waggon towards home suddenly a shout is heard—a crowd comes on—she hears her name called—many voices seem to say "Gustave!"—the crowd gives way.

Well-known eyes are looking into hers as she awakes to consciousness—his arm is round her, and his heart is beating against hers.[31]

Alive, though grievously wounded, he had been taken care of by a noble foe; and at the termination of the war, released, he had come back; one empty sleeve was pinned against his breast, but there she placed the cross,—he smiled fondly on her, but looking at it sighed, thinking perchance glory may be bought too dear.

And now by the Moselle's banks Adèle nurses her invalid husband, and peace for the moment reigns in France. But, alas and alas! many another Adèle will mourn many another Gustave, before mankind have learnt to fulfil the wish contained in Jeanette's song, and be content to

"Let those that make the quarrel be
The only ones to fight."

Reaping.

Toul contains little to detain us except its fine cathedral; it is "dullest of the dull," no movement in its streets; a railroad hurries past her gates, but few of [32] the passengers enter them; her history alone is interesting: built before history for this portion of the globe began, she was, when visited by the Roman eagles, the capital of the warlike Leuci.

Erected at a very early period into a bishopric, its Bishops were its rulers; nominally subject to these Bishops and the Counts of Toul, the burghers seem actually to have enjoyed all the rights of a free city, and eventually the town was reckoned one of the free Imperial cities.

In a quarrel which arose between these burghers and their bishop, Gilles de Sorcy, in the thirteenth century, three arbiters were named to settle the dispute. It appeared, that formerly the townspeople had been obliged to find food for the Bishop's table during the month of April; this custom had fallen into disuse, but now Gilles claimed arrears and its continuance: the burghers, in their turn, claimed certain gifts from the Bishop on his entrance into the city.

It was agreed that the town should pay to the Bishop sixteen pounds, money of Toul, each year; and he, on his part, was to distribute, on his solemn entry into the city, forty measures of wine, eight hundred pounds of bread, and an ox boiled (?) whole, with parsnips.

By this award it would appear that neither party had the upper hand, but that the power was nearly equally divided.

At the death of Gilles dissensions broke out, and in A.D. 1300 the people placed themselves under the protection [33] of the King of France. Disputes now arose between the French monarchs and the German emperors, as Toul was an Imperial free city; but the French were the more active, and the city was considered under their protection.

Occasionally the citizens had to be recalled to a sense of their allegiance by burning their suburbs or occupying their town. Finally, in the sixteenth century, Toul was formally ceded to France, and in A.D. 1700 Louis XIV. pulled down the old walls, and erected the fortifications within which the town now stagnates.

The great canal connecting the Rhine and Marne runs parallel with the Moselle to Frouard, near which place the Meurthe falls in: the country is pleasant, diversified by hill and dale, and richly wooded.

Beyond Liverdun, railroad, road, canal, and river, run side by side,—fire, earth, water, and air, all rendered thus subservient to man.

And now the Meurthe runs in; full of gay confidence, this friend imparts her knowledge to our stream.

She tells her of a city beautifully laid out with gardens of great trees, beneath whose shade gay dames and damsels walk, while music fills the air; hard by the numerous fountains play; and the old palace of King Stanislas, who enriched the town with many a stately building, is near. The shops and cafés, the theatre and walks, all render Nancy a cheerful and agreable abode.[34]

Within the old town is the curious palace of the ancient Dukes, containing a museum, where all sorts of relics are preserved.

Old towers stud the walls; and statues, groves, and churches ornament the town: in the ducal chapel are the tombs of the Dukes of Lorraine, who were powerful sovereign princes. This chapel is very beautiful.

Nancy appears to have been at the height of its lustre during the reign of Stanislas, who received the Duchy of Lorraine, in lieu of his own kingdom of Poland, from the French monarch; at his death the duchy finally reverted to France, and became extinct in 1766.

Stanislas and his queen, in 1699, took part in a very curious ceremony called "The Fête des Brandons," annually practised in Nancy.

This fête was thus conducted: on a certain day all the newly-married couples, of whatever degree, were obliged, under pain of penalty, to go out of the city gate and fetch a fagot; these fagots were, to save them the trouble of going to the wood, sold to them outside the gates, where a sort of fair was held, in which they purchased ribands, pruning-knives of white wood, &c.; they returned, with their fagot bound with the ribands, and the husband with one of the pruning-knives hanging to his button, to the Halle des Cerfs in the ducal palace: from there they went in procession to the market-place, and formed a pile with the fagots; they then inscribed their names at the Hôtel de Ville, in a book kept for that purpose, [35]and received certain privileges for the coming year.

Returning to the palace, they danced in the court, and the young men pelted peas under their feet; which "being," says the chronicler, "very hard, occasioned the dancers many falls, which caused great hilarity among the spectators."

At seven in the evening they had a grand supper at the Hôtel de Ville, and afterwards the bonfire was lit and fireworks sent up.

During the blazing of the bonfire the new-married had the right of proclaiming from the balcony of the Hôtel de Ville, "Les Valentins et les Valentines," *i.e.* they called out the names of any of their unmarried friends with the following words, "Qui donne-t-on à M——?" "Mademoiselle ——" was answered by another, and the crowd took up the names, expressing their approbation or otherwise.

In the course of the next week the Valentin was to send to his Valentine a bouquet, or other present; if she accepted it, she appeared, with the cadeau, at the toilette of the Duchess, on the following Sunday; if no present had been sent by the Valentin, his neighbours lit a fire of straw in front of his house, as a sign of their displeasure.

The ladies were to give a ball to their Valentins, and if they did not do so, a straw-fire was lit before their houses.

These fires were called "Brûler le Valentin," or "Valentine," and showed "the new-married" had made [36]a mistake in their choice for the unmarried. The chronicle finishes by saying, "the people were so pleased at seeing Stanislas and his queen taking a part in their fête, that they did *not* pelt peas under their feet when dancing."

Nancy is not a town of very ancient date like its neighbours, Metz and Toul; it dates only from the eleventh century, and even then it was merely "a castle with a few houses clustered round."

Here Joan of Arc, born at Domremy, near Toul, was first presented by the Sire de Baudricourt to Duke Charles II., who gave her a horse and arms, and sent her to Chinon to the King, Charles VII. of France, to whom Joan made use of the following words:—"Je vous promets de par Dieu, premier qu'il soit un an, tous les Anglais hors de royaume je mettrai, et vous certifie que la puissance en moi est."

After her barbarous murder the King ennobled all her family, males and females, in perpetuity; and they retained this privilege into the seventeenth century, when a parliamentary decree confined the honours to the males.

Many in Lorraine believed that Joan was not really burnt: this belief gave rise to several impostors, one of whom was so successful that she deceived even Joan's brothers, and under her assumed name married a certain Seigneur des Armoises: another was for some time believed in, and fêted accordingly, but at last, being confronted with the King, he posed her by asking what was *the secret* between them.[37]

In 1445 the Duke of Suffolk arrived at Nancy to demand the hand of Marguerite, René's beautiful daughter, for Henry VI. of England; René willingly consented to this honour, and Marguerite went forth to pass her troubled life in camps and battles, until, after the murder of her husband and son, she returned to Lorraine, and died in 1482, near St. Mihiel. She was remarkable, says the historian, for her virtues, her talents, her courage, her misfortunes, and her beauty.

Charles the Bold besieged and took Nancy in 1475; contrary to his usual custom, he was most affable to the citizens, wishing to make Nancy the capital city of the new kingdom he proposed carving out for himself from the adjoining states; but his quarrel with the Swiss arrested the progress of these schemes, and in his absence René II. retook the city, the garrison capitulating: after the capitulation the governor sent René a *pâté* of horseflesh, and told him that for several days they had been reduced to such nourishment.

Immediately afterwards Charles re-appeared, and again besieged the city; René departed to procure assistance from the Swiss, the garrison promising to hold out for two months; and in keeping this promise it suffered great hardships,—the walls were in ruin, a terrible disease appeared within the town, and no less than four hundred men were frozen to death on Christmas night only.

At length René and the Swiss arrived; then the [38] celebrated battle was fought in which Charles was slain. It is said that before the fight commenced he feared for the result, as, in putting on his helmet, the crest fell to the ground. René re-entered his capital by torchlight the same night.

Under its Duke, Charles IV., Nancy suffered much from war, and endured several sieges; at length it was finally incorporated in the French Empire in 1766.

[39]
[Contents]

CHAPTER IV.

Aqueduct at Jouy.

Sweet age of girlhood's prime,
When glad, and gay, and free,
Loving and loved by all,
Life flows on joyously;
Ere yet earth's cares have dimm'd
Eyes bright with happiness,
Or thrown a shade of gloom
O'er the imagined bliss [40]
Of coming life, which in
Dim future seems to shine,
Lit up by present hope
As jewels light the mine.
O fair Moselle! O sweetest Maid!
Who, dancing on midst sun and shade,
Hast left thy distant mountain home,
Through woods and valleys thus to roam;
May no sad shade thy life o'erspread,
No storm break o'er thy beauteous head,
But ever may thy fair wave glide
Peaceful, as when Meurthe's sparkling tide
Flows in, and gently whispering its tale doth tell
To thee, O Queen of Rivers, radiant Moselle!

It is a rich green valley where these waters meet, where the Meurthe dies, and, dying, gives her waters to increase those of her friend.

Bountifully watering the valley's soil, our river flows through the department named after her, Moselle, and forms a large island, where the ancient Roman aqueduct formerly strode over.

Of this aqueduct sixteen arches and one column still remain on the right bank, at the village named Jouy aux Arches; from the gardens above, the river is seen glittering through the valley, which is framed into pictures by the huge arches.

Of course a legend exists that the Devil built this aqueduct. He had promised to do it, for some unknown consideration, before cock-crow; the cock, however, crowed too soon, and the Devil, irritated with the cock and himself, kicked down an unoffending arch: the uncompleted aqueduct soon became ruinous.[41]

Another legend makes Azita (a daughter of Noah) the builder of these arches; she, being a cautious lady, erected them in order that, if another flood came, she might climb up and be safe.

This aqueduct, which was six leagues long, poured its waters into a vast bason, where representations of naval engagements were given by the Romans. It was already a ruin in the tenth century.

Jouy is about six miles from Metz, which is esteemed the strongest city in France, and is garrisoned by twelve thousand men. As we approach the town the beautiful cathedral is seen looming large above the other buildings; it was commenced in the eleventh century, and not completed until the sixteenth: it is elegant in its proportions and beautiful in its detail; another older church is incorporated into it, and its windows are filled with very beautiful stained glass.

Approaching the town, the river breaks into two branches, and another stream comes in, all helping to fortify the old capital of the Austrasians.

The history of Metz is one of the most interesting that can be studied; its first appearance in history is as the capital of the Mediomatrices, and early it became the see of a Christian Bishop.

In the fifth century, Attila with his Huns swept like a pestilence over Europe, and Metz was sacked and burnt; to the Romans, Attila was "the Scourge of God," to his countrymen little less than a god himself. At length he was defeated by the allied Germans and Romans on the plains of Chalons, after losing two [42] hundred thousand men; but even then his power was unbroken, and in a few months he was before Rome, which city he was induced to spare by the intercession of the Pontiff, Leo, who, arrayed in priestly robes and surrounded by his clergy chanting hymns, sought him in his camp. Soon after he retreated northwards, and was murdered by his wife, Criemhilda, who was of German origin: with him fell his vast empire, and the Huns disappeared beyond the Black Sea. This extraordinary century saw the rise and fall of three separate kings and tribes. First came Alaric, king of the Visigoths, who overran the Roman Empire and took Rome itself by storm, A.D. 410; but soon after, dying suddenly, his kingdom perished with him. His body, it is said, was laid in the bed of an Italian river, from which the stream had been diverted; an immense treasure was placed around him, and the stream returning to its natural course, the labourers were murdered, and thus the secret of his burial-place was hid for ever. After him came Attila; and lastly, Odoacer, sprung from the Heruli, became the King of Italy, dethroning Romulus Augustus, the last Roman Emperor: he perished too, being murdered in 493 by orders of Theodoric the Ostrogoth.

During all these wars, and midst the crash of falling empires, rose slowly the sun of Christianity, and soon its penetrating beams dispersed the night that had obscured earth since the Roman splendour had passed away. Now a king was baptized, and anon a martyr died, both events alike serving to spread the religion of[43] peace; and on the ruins of Paganism is now built up the Church of Christ, and a new period of the world's history begins with the downfall of the Roman Empire.

The history of Metz at this early period is the history of the Austrasian kingdom, of which it was the capital.

At the beginning of the fifth century, a nation called the Franks appeared upon the scene of history: this nation was a powerful confederacy of German tribes, and came from the north-western parts of Germany.

They took possession of the neighbouring lands as far as the Moselle, and, the half of them settling on that river, were called the Salii. Gaul soon after being abandoned by the Romans, the Salii became an entirely independent nation, and about A.D. 420, being emulous of the fame of the great Gothic King (Alaric), they for the first time elected a king over themselves, and composed the celebrated Salique law. This king is handed down to us under the name of Pharamond, but it is very doubtful whether such a person ever existed; he was succeeded by Clodion, whose successor, Merowig, was the founder of the Merovingian dynasty: his grandson, Clovis, was the real founder of the kingdom of the Franks; he died "leaving a kingdom more extensive than that of modern France."

He divided his territories into four parts, but his son Clotaire reunited them. Clovis was baptized a Christian in A.D. 493; he was ever the champion of the Church against the great Arian heresy, and has received, therefore, from the Church's hands, a meed of [14] praise, certainly unwarranted, "as he had on all occasions shown himself a heartless ruffian, a greedy conqueror, and a bloodthirsty tyrant;" his great power was only attained by wading through a sea of blood, flowing not only from enemies, but also from his nearest relatives and friends.

Clotaire, who is recorded as having been "cruel and licentious, even for a Merovingian," dying, the kingdom was again divided by his sons into four parts, Sigebert receiving Austrasia, with Metz for his capital.

He married the beautiful Brunhilda, daughter of Athanagildis, king of the Visigoths; and his brother, Chilperic, married her sister: this sister was murdered at the instigation of Fredegunda, to whom Chilperic was shortly after married. Then began a series of murders and bloodshed between the rivals Brunhilda and Fredegunda.

Never, says the historian, has one family amassed such a heritage of crime as King Clovis and his descendants,—the cruelties and murders of his sons were far exceeded by those of his grandsons, their wives, and successors. The history of this period is a chaos of murders, treachery, and license. The kings lived each with several wives and concubines, murdering each other and committing every crime; while the queens caused those who opposed their power to be assassinated, poisoned even their own sons, and sowed dissensions on all sides, leading as vile lives as their husbands. Thus the Merovingian race fell under the weight of its own crimes, and, long before its final [15] extinction in 752, it possessed but the shadow of authority, the real power being in the hands of subjects, termed Mayors of the Palace, who, from being mere house-stewards, rose to be leaders of the armies and presidents of the councils of their effeminate monarchs.

It is curious to find this debased family, through all their misdeeds, crimes, and impotency, still regarded with affection and veneration by the mass of their subjects; and although mere puppets in the hands of the Mayors, the people must have been unaware of their loss of dignity, and their eyes must have been systematically blinded by a fictitious state being preserved round these nominal kings. The following legend of Theolinda will exemplify this; the Sigebert referred to is Sigebert III., son of Dagobert I., who was the last of the family that exercised anything like independent authority.

THEOLINDA.

On the banks of the Moselle, Theolinda was the fairest shepherdess; happy in love and beauty, she sat by the river's bank, Alcidor's arm around her. While sitting thus they were surprised by the approach of Sigebert and his Queen, who were passing a few days in a solitary castle which stood near the banks of the Moselle, surrounded by groves.

The King asked Alcidor if he would wish to serve in the army as a knight's squire; and the Queen offered Theolinda to place her among her ladies, where she [16] would be "as a rose among wild flowers." Both humbly declined, urging that love was sufficient for them, but professed that they were ready to lay down their lives, if needful, for their King: he smiled and left them, assuring them of his protection and assistance, should they need it.

* * *

The hordes of the Vandals were threatening Austrasia, and Sigebert stood on the defensive, feeling his weakness; his general took up a strong position in the Vosges mountains, and there awaited the enemy.

The news of these events reached the quiet valleys of the Moselle, and Alcidor hastened to fulfil his promise to the King, and joined the army that was gathering in the forest of Ardennes; being known as a brave man, and perfectly acquainted with the intricacies of the forest, he was appointed to command a body of bowmen.

A battle ensued, and Alcidor, with his war-cry of "Theolinda," drove all before him, but in the heat of the battle a javelin struck his heart; the battle was lost, and Theolinda heard the news from a grey-haired shepherd: she dropped senseless to the ground, but recovering, hastened to the royal camp.

The King was sitting in his council-chamber, surrounded by his courtiers, in the city of Metz, when a knight came in and said, "Gracious prince! while setting the watch a virgin approached me; she was majestically handsome and mild. First I took her for a divinity, but she addressed me in the following [47] words,—'Permit me to speak to the General before the King quits the council-chamber.'"

"Admit her," quoth the King.

And Theolinda entered, looking mildly and steadfastly around.

"Poor shepherdess!" said the King, "thy faithful lover hath fallen; his memory will ever be dear to us. What can I do for thee?"

"Oh, King," replied Theolinda, "last night I saw him in my dreams, and he told me that by the decree of Heaven I am ordained to stop the career of the barbarian hordes. Wheresoever I cast my looks there shall the dark-red banner fail; the lilies shall advance carried by thy general, I preceding. Thus the white dove shall precede the army and victoriously soar aloft like the royal eagle; and I am come, my King, to lead thy warriors to victory."

The King, without hesitation, exclaimed, "I feel the power of her words, and grant Theolinda's request."

Arrayed in glittering armour, and a white plume on her head, Theolinda preceded the King's army: the King, on a fleet horse, flew from rank to rank encouraging, and victory crowned their efforts; the routed Vandals fled; and peace and prosperity returned to the banks of the Moselle.

Returning in triumph, the festive train proceeded to the Cathedral, and all being assembled within the sacred edifice, the King asked, "Where is the heroic maid that saved the country?"

At these words the ranks of the guards opened, and [48] Theolinda appeared; her arms were bright as the morning-star, her eyes were clear and serious, roses adorned her floating hair. The King addressed her thus: "Be a member of the most noble order; Pharamond's sword knights thee."

The virgin humbly bent her knee, he touched her with his sword, and knights and people shouted, "Hail! all hail! blessed be the saviour of her country!"

One only request she made, which was, that at her death her ashes should be laid with those of the dead Alcidor; and then, heedless of remonstrance, departed to live the life of a hermit in the wilderness; and many suffering pilgrims wandered to her for consolation.

Many years in pious seclusion she lived; at length Alcidor again appeared to her in a dream, and said, "Thy time of probation is ended; follow me now to the regions of eternal bliss!" She inclined her head and died. They laid her, as she had requested, with Alcidor.

In many points of view this legend is curious and interesting; perhaps, could we tear the veil from history, we might find that these Merovingians were not so black as they are painted, or, at any rate, that it was owing to some redeeming points that they lived thus in their subjects' hearts. Curious especially is this legend, inasmuch as in all probability it may have incited Joan of Arc to perform her deeds, the similarity of the two stories being remarkable; and there can be but little doubt that this legend was rife at Joan's day in this [49] district, near which she lived: in any case, the legend is touchingly simple and beautiful; it is given at great length in "Traditions of the Countries of the Rhine," by Dr. Aloys Schreiber.

The Bishops of Metz early played an important part in history. Arnulph, who flourished about 622, was almost a king in power, and from him descended Charles Martel, whose son Pepin became in name, as his father had long been in fact, King of France.

Pepin's son Charlemagne, we are told, held his court at Thionville (about twenty miles lower down the Moselle). Here he was accompanied by his seven beautiful daughters; all taught to work in wool, to ride, and to hunt, in order that they might not be corrupted by idleness: they all supped with him, and when he journeyed rode after him on horseback.

Charlemagne was said to have been seven feet high, and his arm was as mighty as his genius; wisdom and dignity sat on his brow; his seal was the handle of his sword, and he was wont to say, "With my sword I maintain all to which I affix my seal." He died in 814, and was buried sitting upright as on a throne, and clothed in his imperial robes.

His successor, Louis, convoked the States at Thionville in 835; no less than eight Archbishops and thirty-five Bishops attended on this occasion, so numerous had become the Christian prelates. In 869 Charles the Bald was crowned at Metz, the Bishops of Metz and Toul being especially mentioned; [50] and in his grandson's reign we find a Bishop Wala, of Metz, killed before the gates of that city, while fighting bravely in its defence against the Norsemen, who at this period made frequent incursions into France and the adjoining countries. Bishops had ceased to be pastors, and become warriors and temporal princes.

The Bishops of Metz were long able to maintain their authority in the city, though often the citizens disputed it. In Henry the Fowler's reign, Metz became a free imperial city; and in the twelfth century a Maître Échevin, with twelve councillors, was established, and for centuries this form of government was adhered to: thus the Bishops were superseded by a Republic. They still, however, enjoyed considerable power, being the principal parties in the election of the Maître and his council.

A curious legend of Metz is handed down to us from the beginning of the thirteenth century.

THE MIRACULOUS SHIRT.

In Metz there lived a lady named Florentina, whose husband, Alexander, was going to the Crusades; she presented him, on his departure, with a miraculous shirt, which would always retain its purity (a great comfort in a crusade).

The Knight was taken prisoner, and being put to labour, the Sultan remarked the extraordinary circumstance of a prisoner being always in a clean shirt, and [51] inquired the reason. Alexander told him it was a miraculous shirt, which would always remain as spotless as his wife's virtue.

The Sultan despatched a cunning man to undermine the lady's virtue, as he thought ill of the sex.

The emissary was quite unsuccessful.

Florentina having learnt from the cunning man her husband's condition, disguised herself as a pilgrim, and reached the place of his captivity. She then, by her singing, so charmed the Sultan, that, at her request, he made her a present of a slave who she selected. This was her husband; and she gave him his liberty, and received in exchange from him a piece of the miraculous shirt, he not recognising his wife.

Florentina hastened back to Metz, but Alexander arrived there first, and was informed by his friends of his wife's long absence during his captivity. When she arrived, he bitterly reproached her (although the shirt had not become dirty). She explained, and produced the piece he had given her, thus showing how she had been employed; and so they lived happily together.

Very quaint is this legend, and we are at a loss to understand the origin of so curious an invention. The following is a story of the same date, and, though not belonging to Metz, serves to illustrate this period:—

A Thuringian Count, who was married, being taken prisoner in the East, the Sultan's daughter fell in love [52] with him, gave him his liberty, and fled with him to Europe, he promising to marry her.

On arriving at home he presented her to his Countess, and with the consent of all parties, and the Pope's sanction, wedded her also, and they all three lived very happily together. At Erfurt may be seen the three effigies, the Count in the centre: the tombs have been opened, and one of the skulls was found to be like an Asiatic's, thus in some measure corroborating the truth of this remarkable tale.

Metz.

17

We have now emerged from what may be termed the ancient history of Metz, and the more detailed accounts of the modern period give us a series of [53]sieges, battles, and plots, from which we will select those appearing the most interesting.

In 1354 the Emperor Charles IV. remained some time at Metz, and returned there again two years after, when he held a Diet, at which the Archbishops of Trèves, Cologne, and Mayence, and the four lay-Electors, were present. At this Diet additions were made to the celebrated Golden Bull, which was then published, and remained the law of the Empire until the nineteenth century. Metz was now at the height of its glory. Now, say the "Annals," Metz was resplendent with knights, princes, dukes, and archbishops. The Emperor, clothed with the imperial ensigns, and surrounded by the great officers of state, the naked sword in his hand and the crown on his head, attended service in the Cathedral.

A party in the town wished to raise a tumult, and deliver the city to the Emperor; but the Cardinal de Piergort representing the infamy of such treachery, the Emperor sent for the chiefs of the city and gave up to them the traitors, who, when night-time came, were drowned in the river. The Emperor departed, and then followed a series of discords unimportant except to the actors.

In 1365, companies of countrymen, and pillagers set free by the peace of Bretigny, succeeded each other in attacking Metz, and ravaging the neighbourhood. With some difficulty they were defeated and dispersed.

No sooner were these petty wars ended, than a [54]larger one broke out with the Lorrainese; and the Count de Bar advanced to Metz and defied the Messins to combat, sending them a bloody gauntlet. The citizens, however, declined the conflict, and peace was concluded.

In 1405 an *émeute* took place in the town, and the people rising turned out the magistrates, and replaced them with their own representatives. Soon, however, the ancient rulers managed to reinstate themselves, and took a bloody vengeance on their enemies.

In 1407, the Duke de Bar resolved to take Metz by surprise. He secretly fitted out a train of boats, filled with arms and munitions of war, and sent a large body of soldiers, who secreted themselves near the town. All was prepared, and on the morrow an attack was to be made, when a sudden panic seized the attacking party, and they fled, leaving their boats and munitions, by which the Messins learnt the peril they had escaped.

In 1444, a furious war was waged between the Duke of Lorraine and the Messins: the Duke was assisted by his brother-in-law, Charles VII. of France. The quarrel originated in some money claims that the city had on the Duchess of Lorraine, which claims she refused to satisfy. The irritated Messins seized on the lady's baggage between Pont-à-Mousson and Nancy, as she was performing a pilgrimage to the former. The Duke, in revenge, besieged the city, and the burghers ravaged his territories. Much blood was shed on both sides, until at last peace was made [55]between the belligerents by the King, who received a sum of money from the Messins. So powerful was this republic, that it could single-handed wage war with a sovereign prince.

A few years after, when the celebrated War of Investitures took place, the Messins were called on to fight for Adolphe of Nassau, the nominee of the Pope. They pleaded their privileges and the late ruinous wars, and begged to remain neutral. The Pope, in consequence, excommunicated the city; a great number of the clergy obeyed the Papal Bull, and left in procession for Pont-à-Mousson, with the cross and banners at their head. For three years this extraordinary state of things lasted, during which time the churches were empty and the dying unshriven. At length the Pope took off the interdict, and the priests and canons returned, but the Messins had to pay dearly for their opposition to ecclesiastical power.

About this period the wily Louis XI. of France thought the time was come for joining Metz to his dominions; he accordingly wrote a kind, mild letter to the citizens, suggesting that they should put themselves under his protection, and thus secure their peace. The citizens wrote back cautiously, but expressed their surprise at the King's proposition; he, fearing to incense and thus throw so powerful a city into alliance with the noblesse that were taking part against him, disowned his herald, and denied the letter he had sent.

18

The next event was an endeavour to take Metz by [50]storm, on the part of the Duke of Lorraine, and it very nearly succeeded. Early in the morning of the 9th April, 1473, while the Messins still slept, ten thousand Lorrainese arrived near the walls from Pont-à-Mousson, having marched during the night; with them was a certain Krantz, nicknamed "La Grande Barbe," who had constructed a peculiar waggon, filled with casks, which was capable of sustaining the weight of a portcullis, and thus preventing its closing when once it had been raised.

Disguised as merchants, Krantz and some of his companions, with a train of waggons filled with casks, among which was the peculiarly-constructed one, appeared before the city gates, and were admitted; the waggons entered, and the particular one was halted immediately beneath the portcullis, the pretended merchants then rushed on the guardian of the gate and killed him.

Being joined by a select body of five hundred men, who quickly entered, La Grande Barbe raised the shout of "Ville gagnée!" adding, "Slay, slay, women and children; spare none! Vive Lorraine!"

The awakened burghers rushed in disorder from their beds, knowing what these sounds portended, and all was lost but for the presence of mind of a baker named Harelle, who lived near the gate under which the waggon was stationed. He ran to the house over the gate, and succeeded in lowering the side portions of the portcullis, so that horsemen could not enter, and foot soldiers only by creeping under the waggon. [52]

Then rushing into the streets, Harelle rallied and encouraged the citizens, and finally routed the Lorrainese, slaying La Grande Barbe and two hundred of his companions, the rest escaping by flight.

In a few minutes all was over; the assaulters dead or flown, the gates reclosed, and the assembled Council preparing to prosecute the war. Thus the clear-headed baker saved the good city of Metz.

In 1473 the Emperor Frederick III. visited the town, and the keys being presented to him, he promised solemnly to preserve the liberties of the citizens. He then, accompanied by his son, Maximilian, entered in state, followed by the Archbishop of Mayence, and other princes and prelates.

The Messins had been so harassed by attempts at surprise that they now were ever on their guard against them; and so fearful had they become, that when the Emperor, in visiting their church, came to the great bell, and expressed a wish to hear it sound, they declined respectfully, saying it was an old custom only to sound it thrice in the year. This they did, fearing it might be meant as a signal of attack on their hardly-maintained liberties. They also had, during the Emperor's visit, 2000 men constantly under arms, ready to obey the Maître Echevin's orders at a moment's notice; and they kept strict guard over the gates.

While Frederick was with them the Messins refused to admit Charles the Bold, with more than five hundred horsemen. He was furious, but the Emperor agreed to meet him at Trèves instead; and afterwards Duke [58]Charles had no time or opportunity to revenge himself on Metz, but rather conciliated that powerful city, and when he took Nancy sent a present of cannon and other spoil to the Messins, who were delighted at the misfortune of their old enemies, the Lorrainese.

In 1491 another attempt was made by the Duke of Lorraine to gain possession of the town. Surprise and stratagem having previously failed, he now tried treachery, and secured the services of a certain Sire Jehan de Landremont, who induced one of the gatekeepers, named Charles Cauvellet, a Breton by birth, but who had acquired the rights of citizenship, to join the plot.

All was easily arranged, thanks to Cauvellet, who had the keys of the city. A day was fixed on, but it turning out so rainy that the river flooded the approaches to the town, a fresh day was named; in the meantime Cauvellet's conscience pricked him, and he confessed the plot to the Maître Echevin. His life was spared, but the Sire de Landremont, after his sentence had been read at every cross-street in the town, he being led about on horseback for this purpose, was strangled, drawn, and quartered. He died with a smile on his countenance, saying he only regretted having been unsuccessful.

A peace was soon after patched up between René and the Messins.

19

Though so long resisting, the city was doomed eventually to fall by treachery, and the time at length arrived.[59]

In 1552, Henry II. of France entered Lorraine, and occupied Pont-à-Mousson. On the 10th of April he presented himself before the gates of Metz, which is styled in the annals of the day "a great and rich imperial city, very jealous of its liberties." Although Henry had taken the most rigorous measures to suppress Protestantism in his own dominions, he here appeared as the champion of that religion, and entered into a secret treaty with the Protestant Princes, who agreed that he should occupy Metz, Courtrai, Toul, and Verdun, as Vicar-Imperial. Henry, wishing to gain immediate possession of Metz, engaged his ally, the Bishop, to bribe the inhabitants of the "Quartier du Heu," and raise dissensions among the garrison. These preparations made, the Sieur de Tavannes arrived before that quartier, and harangued the people, telling them that the good King Henry was fighting for their liberties, and they could not do less than allow him to lodge in their town with his body-guard of five hundred men. "Surely that was not too much to grant to their defender?" The people, half-persuaded, allowed a body of men to approach and commence filing through the gate, but seeing that instead of five hundred there were nearly five thousand drawing near, they wished to close the gate; but Tavannes continued to speak them fair until upwards of seven hundred picked men had entered, when a Swiss captain, who held the keys for Metz, seeing the number, threw the keys at Tavannes' head, exclaiming in the idiom of the country, "Tout est choué."[60]

Thus was Metz taken, kings and nobles thinking any treachery fair against mere bourgeois. Of course Henry kept it for himself, not the Protestant interest; and henceforward it remained a portion of the French dominions.

Before the Emperor Charles V. allowed so important a free city quietly to revert to France, he sent Alba with a large army to besiege it, he remaining at Thionville to watch proceedings, his health being too bad to allow him to prosecute the siege in person.

The town was defended by the young Duke of Guise, who turned out all the women, old men, and children, and pulled down half the town in order the better to defend the other half; working himself in the trenches, he by his example so encouraged his soldiers and citizens, that they sustained all the assaults of the Imperialists.

Charles V., seeing that the siege did not progress, and that the breaches were repaired as fast as made; finding also that his own army was rapidly wasting with cold and sickness, reluctantly ordered Alba to raise the siege; the Duke retired, leaving his tents and sick, together with a great quantity of baggage and munitions: to the credit of the conquerors, they treated the sick with great kindness, contrary to the usual custom at that period. Charles departed, saying that he perceived "Fortune, like other women, accorded her favours to the young, and disdained grey locks."

In 1555, the people of Metz became exceedingly [61]discontented at the Governor's taking-away many of their ancient liberties; this gave rise to the

[Contents]

PLOT OF THE CORDELIERS.

A Cordelier, named le Père Léonard, guardian of a convent, engaged many of the leading townspeople in a conspiracy to retake Metz from the French.

For this purpose, having first persuaded his brother monks to join him, he introduced into the convent, which had walls capable of defence, arms and soldiers.

He then agreed with the Governor of Thionville to open an entrance into the town for a body of Imperialist troops on a given night; at the same time, to distract the French, the town was to be fired in several places.

Vieilleville, the Governor of Metz, hearing that a Cordelier was constantly seen in conversation with the Governor of Thionville, became suspicious, and suddenly visiting the convent, found the arms and concealed men; he also seized Père Léonard as he entered the city on his return from Thionville, and learning from him that a body of Imperial troops was to march to Metz that very night, despatched a force, which, taking them by surprise, routed them and cut them to pieces.

The monks, from whom by promises and threats he had extorted a full disclosure of the plot, he threw into a dungeon, telling them they should be hanged next day, and might confess to each other.[62]

On the dungeon being opened in the morning, it was found that the monks, enraged with the Superior, who had drawn them into the plot, had killed him and maimed his four advisers; these latter were, with ten of their brethren, hanged, and the ten youngest were exiled from the town.

In 1631, Metz capitulated to Gustavus Adolphus; he remained there all the winter, and presented the Bishop's library to his Chancellor, Oxenstiern, who sent it off to Sweden; but the vessel sank and the books were lost.

The only other extract from the history of Metz we shall here give is of a different character.

Louis XV. arrived at Metz with a strong army, in order to oppose Charles of Lorraine, whose duchy he had given to Stanislas of Poland.

Louis, who was accompanied by his mistress, the Duchess of Châteauroux, and her sister, was taken mortally ill; previously there had been erected a wooden gallery, which led, along the sides of four streets, from the Duchess's apartments to those of the King: this gallery was now given up at the angry remonstrances of the people, who were much scandalized by the proceedings, and the sisters proceeded to the King's residence, where they shut themselves into an apartment adjoining that of the dying monarch.

The Duke de Richelieu, who was in league with the Duchess, was First Lord of the Bedchamber, and [63]would not allow any of the Princes to have access to the King.

The town urged the King's Confessor to remonstrate with him, but he refused; then the Bishop of Soissons undertook the task, and threatened the King that he would not administer the last sacrament to him if he refused to dismiss his mistresses. The doors were thrown open between the King's room and that where the Duchesses sat, anxiously waiting the turn of events.

At length the King was induced to order them to depart, and they fled into the country.

Contrary to all expectation, and in consequence of a strong dose administered by a quack, the King recovered, after he had been given over by his doctors and received the last sacrament. The Duchesses were recalled.

Metz at the present day is the chief town of the Department of the Moselle; it is situated on both banks and the island formed by the embranchment of the river: its picturesque streets are connected by several bridges, from which the views are very striking.

It has excellent bathing establishments, fine cafés, a theatre, good shops, and above all a promenade, almost unequalled in beauty; it is situated on very high ground, densely shaded with great trees: seats, and flowers, and grass are there; the military bands play in the evening; the ladies are handsome and well-dressed, [64]and from the walks the view extends for many miles over the green plains of the Moselle; the different branches of the river shine in the valley; the sun sets over the hills which westward bound the view, its golden light streams through the foliage and suffuses the whole valley; little boats glide up and down the stream; merry voices sing in the distance; and thus, with music, beauty, and sunshine, we leave the old Austrasian capital.

Environs of Metz.

[65]
[Contents]

CHAPTER V.

Roman Bridge at Trèves.

Leaving Metz, and all its soldiers, ramparts, and ditches far behind, our river, passing through a level country, arrives at Thionville. This town was in the diocese of Trèves, and dependent on the Parliament of Metz. Here Charlemagne had a favourite palace; and here, in a solemn assembly, he parted his vast estates between his three sons.

Its history is like that of Metz, made up of sieges, [66]assaults, and surprises, but of less importance and less interest. It was always a strong place, and at the present day its fortifications, constructed by Vauban and Cormontaigne, are amongst the strongest in Europe: it lies in a level plain, and is uninteresting, though rather picturesque.

The Moselle rolls on, and in about twelve miles reaches Sierck, a clean little town, on its right bank; and then we pass from France to Prussia, and our river becomes German, its future beauty beginning to dawn as it approaches Trèves. Two streams here increase the volume of her waters—a smaller one on the left, and the Saar on the right.

There is one peculiar charm about the banks and neighbourhood of the Moselle, found equally at its source near Bussang, and amidst the German hills, this is, the number and variety of the beautiful wild-flowers with which its whole course teems, and with which our river is, as it were, garlanded.

MOSELLE FLOWERS.
Where the Mosell murmurs low,
As its waters gently flow
Through the woods and flow'ry dells,
There a wood-nymph hidden dwells.
Hidden she from mortal view,
Yet her footsteps may be traced
Where the night has scattered dew.
And the boughs are interlaced.
[67]
If her feet have pressed the ground,
There the blooming flowers are found;
These gifts mark where she has strayed,—
Thus we trace the fairy maid.
The violet and lily grow.
The wild-rose and the tiny pink.
And the brilliant corn-flowers blow.
Hard by the gentle river's brink;
The foxglove waves its lofty head
Above the trickling streamlet's bed;
The wild convolvulus doth twine
Its graceful arms around the vine.
The snapdragon and mignonette.
The clematis and flox,
In ev'ry vale are frequent met;
And springing from the rocks,
The broom, the fern, and sweet red heather.
Profuse are found in groups together.
The raspberry, strawberry, and thyme,
Over every hill do climb;
And in ev'ry wild retreat
We find the honeysuckle sweet.
Blackberries, with fruit and thorn,
With the wild hop intertwine;
All these flowers the woods adorn,
And their loveliness combine.
So the wood-nymph's steps we trace,
As she roams from place to place,
Scattering beauty o'er the ground;
Thus the earth with flowers is crowned.

Only a few of the flowers that we find growing there are enumerated in the above; moreover, they are more beautiful than wild flowers usually are, attaining [68]to great size;

the enothera, harebells, and campanulas, with wild geraniums, and a host of others, go to swell the list.

Before the Saar runs in, the red rocks of Trèves appear on the left bank, jutting over the trees, close to the river's course; then they retire inland, until the old Roman bridge is reached; there they again approach, and from their heights the remnant of old Trèves is spread out, environed by its avenues and studded with its churches and ruins. The river is beneath; and the eight-arched bridge, complete as in the golden days of Rome, clasps the waist of our river as a zone encircling that of a young girl just budding into womanhood.

And so, our graceful woman-stream at Trèves ceases her girlhood and becomes more beautiful, more reflective, and more graceful; the hills draw near, and the vineyards sparkle among the rocks; her handmaidens, the brooks, wait at every turn to tend her, increasing her beauty; and following in her train, pass along in glorious procession, the trees bending and the rocks falling back before the might of innocence and love.

Strong in innocence, with virgin bosom unsullied, nothing less bright than heaven's reflection ever having rested there; but mightier still in love,—abounding love,—that causes her to feed the earth and fertilise the soil wherever she passes; so that man, receiving at her hands his daily food, thanks and blesses her, and praises, through her, her Creator.

We, the lookers-on, or lighter toilers, should bless her surely not less than the poor vine-dresser or digger [62] of the soil. True, for one she has carved the rock into sunny platforms, and for the other she has left upon the rocks a thick coating of productive earths; but to us she has given that brighter gift of higher value far,—the impress of God's beneficence, not merely through material food and drink, but through the superior senses which feed the mind.

It is impossible to wander from the source of our Moselle, to muse over the rise and fall of the nations and cities on her banks, to look upon her rocks and flowers, to glide adown her stream, to stand amidst the ruined walls of her old towers, to watch the seed-time and harvest on her banks, the clustering bunches and the brilliant glow of the wine and corn, with all the lesser incidents adorning her;—it is impossible to view all these, to ruminate and gaze, to live with her and be of her in all her windings, all her sunshine and refreshing shade, and not imbibe a portion of her spirit; a portion, larger as we look deeper and think more, of her innocence and peace of mind, which, laid up within our hearts, as the corn and wine within the store, will give us at a future time joy and gladness.

Harvest-time passes, and the vintage ends; but when the long winter comes, their productiveness is present, and the stores laid up are found to be indeed true treasures. [70]

1 German name for the Moselle.

[Contents]

CHAPTER VI.

"Augusta Trevirorum" of the Romans, "Trier" of the Germans, and "Trèves" to English, is, or at any rate claims to be, the most ancient city of Europe; according to the legend it was founded by a Prince Trebeta, who was driven out of his Asiatic possessions by Semiramis. He is described as having been a wise and strong prince, who built a magnificent palace of vast strength on the heights over the Moselle, opposite to the town, which he called after his own name: these things he did 1300 years before the foundation of Rome; and on the "Rothen Haus" in Trèves are still the words, "*Ante Romam Treviris stetit annis mille trecentis.*" A picture, said to represent this Prince Trebeta, is in the Town-hall: he is sitting [ ] on his father's lap, with the spires of the Cathedral in his hand.

Very interesting is Trèves; and if we cannot place confidence in Prince Trebeta and his days, we must turn to that surer period when it was the capital of the Roman dominions beyond the Alps, and received the name of Augusta of the Trevii; these Trevii being the German tribe residing around this part of the Moselle.

Under its Roman name Trèves rose to the height of its glory; it was then celebrated for the number of its magnificent temples, its splendid palaces, its amphitheatre and baths. Remnants of this past splendour still exist; such as portions of the baths and amphitheatre, the bridge, and especially the Porta Nigra, which is one of the finest Roman ruins extant.

Porta Nigra.

Trèves was frequently the residence of the Roman Emperors, and its inhabitants had all the privileges of [72]Roman citizenship. In the last half of the third century Galienus held his court here; and here Maximian was attacked by the Franks, whom he defeated. Here Constantine the Great, when celebrating a victory that he had gained over the Franks, caused two of the captive princes to be thrown to wild beasts in the arena. They met their death with smiles, and shortly after the whole of the German nation rose to avenge them. Constantine disguised himself, and entering the hostile camp, gave the enemy false information, which led to their total defeat, A.D. 310. The simple-minded Germans were no match for the Romans in fraud; they deemed any ambuscade, or advantage taken against an enemy, dishonourable, and we even find them sending messages to their opponents of the day and hour upon which they intended to attack them.

The cruelty of throwing captives to wild beasts, however, we find surpassed by a German named Magnentius, who, having become a Roman soldier, set himself up for Emperor in opposition to Constantius. This Magnentius, on the eve of the great battle of Marsa, sacrificed a maiden, and mixing her blood with wine, gave his army to drink, and invoked his gods, pouring a libation of this fiendish drink in their honour. He was totally defeated, and killed himself.

The Western Empire of the Romans fell, and Germans walked the streets of Rome, supplanting with their fresh vigour the worn-out strength of that wonderful empire, on the ruins of which their leaders planted their feet, which at first slipped and stumbled, but [73]eventually found a firm basis, on which was erected what we call Modern History.

Many legends are given us by the German poets connected with Trèves; the following are the most remarkable:—

LEGEND OF THE GREAT CANAL FROM TRÈVES TO COLOGNE.

For more than a hundred years the people of Cologne had been endeavouring to raise a Cathedral that should eclipse all others. The master-builder was busy making measurements for the arch of the great door, when one of his apprentices jeeringly said the building would never be finished, but ever remain in fragments. Thereupon the master waxed wroth and dismissed the apprentice, who departed, saying: "Woe to thee, O my master! never shall thy work be finished; sooner shall I complete a canal from here to Trier, than shalt thou place a tower upon thy cathedral."

Years passed on, and the Cathedral was rapidly approaching to completion, when the master saw a huge worm creep from the ground. This was the fiend, by whose assistance the apprentice had made a canal from Trèves to Cologne: the apprentice appeared to the astonished master and said, "Lo, my canal is complete, while thy church is yet a fragment!" and water flowed from the canal, on which a duck came swimming from Trèves.[74]

The water rose and encompassed the master, who thus perished, and his cathedral is still unfinished; but the wicked apprentice fared still worse, for the great worm strangled him, and he is doomed evermore to haunt the cathedral, measuring the uncompleted works.

The canal thus formed was used to send wine from Trèves to Cologne, without the trouble of putting it into casks.[1]

Not less wonderful is the following:—

LEGEND OF THE DOM[2] OF TRÈVES.

While meditating over his undertaking, the contractor for the building of the Dom was accosted by a gentlemanlike stranger in red, who said to him in a hearty tone, "Cheer up, for I can help you; but first tell me for what purpose you wish so large a house."

The contractor, delighted, guessed who the stranger was, and replied in artful words that he wished to raise this house for a gambling and drinking palace.

"Hurrah!" said the man in red, "just what I am fond of!" and they agreed upon terms and went to work.[75]

24

The building went bravely on, until the Red Man seeing altars and such-like things arising, with which he was then unacquainted, asked what it all meant; but being told that these were tables for dice, was satisfied.

One day, returning from the roof to which he had been carrying up large stones, the Red Man saw the Bishop consecrating the new church; then the bells tolled solemnly, and Satan found he had been outwitted. He rushed at an altar, and endeavoured to tear it down, but left a claw sticking into it, it having been consecrated; then with a yell he fled, and the contractor mocked him, shouting "Never build more churches without a written agreement."

The conversion of the heathen Trevii to Christianity was, according to the legend, thus effected:—

The people of Trèves worshipped a statue of marble, from whose mouth oracles proceeded; troops of pilgrims came to Trèves to hear from this idol's lips answers to their questions: but now a foreign priest appeared before the crowd, and with a crucifix in his hand he spoke to them of Christ the Son of God; the people, leaving their idol for the Truth, flocked to his feet, in spite of the threats of the heathen priests.

Thus Saint Eucharius converted the Trevii.

* * *

The Moselle country was especially resorted to by hermits, who lived in recesses of the mountains; of these Saint Antony was the first.[76]

Saint Nicolas was the patron of the bridge, and his statue stands beneath the stone crucifix which adorns it. On one occasion, a mariner, whose ship was in great danger of being cast away beneath the bridge, called on the Saint, and vowed an offering of a taper as big as his mast should he escape.

He landed in safety, but finding himself secure snapped his fingers at the Saint, saying, "Nicolas, thou wilt not have so much." The Saint replied not.

Again this mariner's vessel coming down the stream was in danger of the bridge; once more he cried on Nicolas, but the water checked his cry, and man and ship were lost.

There is another legend of the Moselle bridge, which we will call—

[Contents]

THE RING.

A certain man of noble family, after leading a glorious life, committed fratricide; repenting of his crime he left his country, and after many years arrived at Trèves.

At sunset he stood upon the Moselle bridge, and there, kneeling before the crucifix, wept; his tears flowing into the stream beneath: an Angel swept by, and left him a palm-twig from heaven. He exultingly cried, "Lord, forgive my sins before my end—never will I cease to repent my grievous sin;" then, throwing his ring, which he had taken from his [ ] brother, into the river, he prayed that if he were forgiven it should be returned to him.

Rising, he retired into a monastery, and eventually became a Bishop. A fisherman one day arrived and offered him a fish; he took it, thinking it a mark of reverence.

At dinner the cook approached and presented him with a ring, which he had found within the fish.

The Bishop perceived it was his own, and exclaiming, "Heaven has sent it to me as a proof of forgiveness!" expired.

[Contents]

THE CRUCIFIX IN THE MARKET-PLACE.

In the market-place at Trèves there stands a column, with a crucifix on its summit. An inscription on it gives the following miracle as the cause of its erection.

The Huns were swarming over Germany, burning and destroying all things: their march was as a pestilence; but the people of Trèves were gay and merry, as if no danger threatened,—they rioted in wine, and luxury.

One man only, within the city, still remained sober and prudent, and he dreamt that he saw a great monster descending from the Marcusberg and crawling its hideous length towards Trèves; arriving at the Moselle, the loathsome monster rolled into its blue waves, and caused them so to swell that the city was overflowed.[78]

Awaking, this good man ran to the Archbishop and told his dream, explaining its meaning to be that the Huns were marching on the city by the Marcusberg; the Archbishop only laughed at him, at which he grew angry: but soon better thoughts possessed him, and he prayed Heaven to avert the impending ruin.

The sky grew black and dreadful; a nameless horror came upon the people, and falling down they implored pardon for their sins, and crosses fell from heaven.

Then, believing, they marched out to the Marcusberg, and finding the Huns vanquished them.

Two new powers arose in Europe during the last days of the Roman Empire: the one, as we have before said, planted its feet on the ruins of Imperial Rome, and henceforth wielded her temporal authority,—this was the German, or Frankish power; the other, amidst the fallen temples overthrown by the German conquerors, raised up a fairer temple and a purer worship,—this was the Church of Christ. At first over-shadowed by the more gorgeous worship and grander temples of the false gods of Paganism, the new Church had to struggle for a mere existence; but these being overthrown, the remnants of Paganism soon melted away before the innate majesty of truth, and the fanes of superstition crumbling into dust, afforded a sure foundation for the new and mightier edifice.[79]

These two powers, at the extinction of the Western Empire, ruled nearly the whole of Europe: neither was as yet concentrated, both had many heads, and it was not until the two powers coalesced that either attained that temporal influence which they have since possessed. Hand in hand, we find these two powers progressing in might and influence; sometimes a temporary quarrel would separate, but common interest invariably reunited them.

It is in its infancy that the Church of Christ shines with its purest light; and it is, consequently, to this period that the mind loves to revert, and dwell on "that happy spring time" when the Fathers of the Church went forth among the heathen, gathering the nations into one family, the centre and head of which was God. How wonderful to watch "the little star appearing in the East," and rising over the ruins and decaying temples of old Rome, till gradually the whole air was filled with the "light of truth!"

Alas! that a time should come when, waning from its throne on high, the Church fell so low in the person of its ministers and adherents, that we find the chroniclers of the fifteenth century recording that "Nuns did what the Devil was ashamed to think; and that Abbots, by means of their *poverty*, became the greatest proprietors; of their *obedience*, mighty princes; and of their *chastity*, husbands of all women;" and we hear of men complaining that they were not rich enough to become monks.

It is needless, however, here to give an account of [80]those vicious customs that arose within the bosom of the Church of Rome, and eventually caused what we have quoted; we will rather turn to the legends of the earlier period, many of which are singularly beautiful. Among them we shall find many things which at first sight may provoke a smile, but on reflection we shall arrive at the meaning of what must be taken merely as an allegory.

For instance, we are told that "King Sigebert appointed St. Goar to the Bishopric of Trèves, and the Saint entering the King's saloon, hung his cloak over a sunbeam, to prove that he was enlightened by God." This would probably be an illustration of the power of faith, and so with the other legends of the time. Here we shall only select a few that are immediately connected with Trèves.

LEGEND OF ORENDEL.3

The great King Eigel resided at Trèves. He was supreme over twelve kingdoms; his favourite son was Orendel.

Orendel having reached his thirteenth birth-day was invested with a sword, and vowed before the Virgin to be "a true chevalier on earth, and a defender of widows and orphans;" then proceeding to his father, he begged of him a wife, that the kingdom might have a queen.[81]

His father told him there was none in all his kingdoms worthy to be his spouse; but at Jerusalem there lived a beautiful Queen, Breide by name, to whom the holy grave belonged: her he must seek, and could he succeed in wedding her, his happiness would be complete.

Orendel, transported with the account of this virgin queen, prayed his father to prepare him ships. His father consented, and three years were spent in preparing for the expedition.

Then in a great assembly the young King, who wished none but volunteers to go with him on his journey, spake aloud: "Where are ye, O courageous Kings! who will risk with me the voyage to the Holy Tomb?" and eight brave kings stepped out, each with a thousand knights.

Again King Orendel spake out: "Where are ye, Dukes and Counts! who will join me in my voyage for the honour of God and the Holy Tomb?" and a thousand nobles offered.

Once more spake Orendel: "Be warned, O Kings, and Knights, and Nobles! ye will suffer hell's heat and distress before ye reach the Tomb. Come not unwillingly, nor unarmed." Nothing daunted, all girded their swords, and prepared for the long journey.

Thus went King Orendel forth from Trèves, surrounded by his kings and knights, a golden cross grasped firmly in his hand, and the people cheering. Embarking, he was carried by the Moselle upon [82]his course, and in the Holy Land he found his "Breide."

[Contents]

THE GREAT MASSACRE.

Varus, the governor of Gaul, caused so many Christians to be massacred in Trèves that the Moselle ran red with blood, until it reached Neumagen. For this he was condemned to ramble restlessly about the city after his death, and to do deeds of kindness, assisting every one requiring his aid in Trèves. In this character he is called "the City Ghost."

In after days a penitent from Trèves sought absolution from the Pope. The latter ordered him to fetch a piece of earth from Trèves; and on the penitent's again presenting himself with the earth, the Holy Father prayed, and pressed it in his hands, and blood dropped therefrom immediately.

"This blood," said the Holy Father, "was shed by martyrs in Trèves, who loved Christ so heartily that they gave their lives for him, and thus became protectors of their city.

"Go; thou art absolved for their sakes. And tell thy people what thou hast seen and heard, that so they may be increased in their faith."

[Contents]

ST. MATERN.

St. Matern was the first Bishop of Cologne, and [83]was much beloved. He died young, and the mourning people sent to Rome to pray St. Peter for comfort.

St. Peter gave a staff to the emissaries, and bid them beat upon the earth where Matern's bones were laid; at the same time they were to call on him to rise, as it was not yet time for him to rest, but he must still combat for the sake of God.

This was done; and Matern, who had been dead forty days, arose, and administered three bishoprics at once; viz. Tongern, Trèves, and Cologne.

[Contents]

THE FIRST FOUNDLING HOSPITAL.

The first institution of this nature is said to have been in Trèves, and was thus established: Saint Goar was a very pious man, harming none, but the wicked calumniated him to the Bishop of Trèves.

The Bishop ordered him to appear before him, and, to test his power, asked him to declare who was the father of a child that had been exposed near the Cathedral.

The Saint bending prayed, and touched the child's lips; whereon the child spoke, and the uttered word was "Rusticus," which was the Bishop's name.

The Bishop grew pale, the calumniators slunk away, and St. Goar, turning to the Bishop, said, "Perceivest thou not thy duty? As the Church embraces with tender arms erring children, so must thou, the head [84]of thy Church, foster such poor children, and bring them up in the fear of God."

Roman Baths.

27

The city of Trèves and surrounding country fell under the sway of the Archbishops of the diocese, who were usually more warriors than priests, if we may judge by their acts. Here is a picture of a brother-Archbishop, who flourished in 1169:—"Christian of Mayence is said to have spoken six languages, and was celebrated for his knightly feats of arms. He was daily to be seen with a golden helmet on his head, armed cap-à-pié, and mounted on his war-horse, the archiepiscopal mantle floating from his [85] shoulders, and in his hand a heavy club, with which he had brained thirty-eight of his enemies."

There were at this time four orders of nobility:—the Ecclesiastical, comprising Bishops, Abbots, and other Church dignitaries. The remaining three orders may be classed as follows:—

First, the old and proud families who still retained their free grants of lands; these despised alike Princes and Bishops, Court and Ecclesiastical dignitaries.

The second order was formed of the nobles belonging to the different orders of knighthood; these collectively enjoyed the power of individual princes.

The remaining order consisted of the feudal aristocracy; these were the court nobility, who filled all the offices of state, and although bound by oath to support their princes, they were often leagued together in arms against them.

These four powers were in constant hostility, and from the skirts of the second and last crept forth a fifth disturbing force; this was made up of what are ordinarily termed the Robber-Knights, the ruins of whose castles are frequent on the Moselle and Rhine. In consequence of their depredations, the princes and nobles were forced to erect strongholds to protect their towns and villages; hence arose the numerous towers whose ruins adorn the banks of the Moselle and other rivers.

Most of the later legends are connected with these Robber-Knights; and the history of their petty wars with the Archbishops of Trèves and the Counts of [86] Sponheim (the latter being lords of a large tract of country), is the history of the Moselle during the middle ages.

The Counts of Sponheim, too, were generally at variance with the Archbishops of Trèves, and both these powers with the Archbishops of Cologne; so we plainly see the necessity of the walls, which still exist in fragments round the old towns and villages; and while we quietly sketch the picturesque gate and water-towers, our minds revert to the days when the poor burghers guarded them with jealousy.

The burghers eventually, however, carried the day; and as they increased in power the Robber-Knights were gradually swept away, leaving only the blackened walls of their old keeps to mark where they had plied their trade of robbery. See in the following story how the citizens of Trèves paid off a certain Robber-Knight, named Adalbert, whose castle was situated near their town, meeting violence with fraud.

[Contents]
THE ANIMATED WINE-CASKS.

Adalbert, from his castle of Saint Cross, disturbed by robbery the city of Trèves. The city swore vengeance.

A certain brave knight, named Sicco, offered to destroy both Adalbert and his castle by cunning. This offer was gladly accepted, and the clergy blessed the cunning knight.

* * *

[87]
On a very hot day, when all within the Saint Cross castle were dozing, a stranger appeared at the gate, and begged the warder to give him a cup of wine, as he had travelled far, being just arrived from Italy, and was on his way to his castle on the Moselle.

The refreshment was given him, and the grateful traveller requested the warder to tell his master that his kindness would not be unrewarded, as he was the owner of a fair vineyard, and when he arrived at home he would send him some casks of his best wine in return for his hospitality.

Before long a troop of peasants were seen approaching the castle, escorting several carts laden with casks, which, however, were filled with armed men instead of strong wine.

The warder challenged the procession, and Sicco, who was disguised as a peasant, said that they were sent by the pilgrim to whom Adalbert had been so hospitable, and who now forwarded them in conformity with his word.

The door was opened, and Adalbert himself conducted the carts into the court-yard; then Sicco drew his sword, and gave the signal to his followers by slaying Adalbert, and the men, being liberated from the casks, rushed on the garrison and slew them all; then the castle was burnt. On the ruins a church was built.

The Crusades gave a new impetus to arts and sciences, bringing the luxury and refinement of the [88]East into contact with the almost barbaric simplicity of the Western nations; and from the eleventh century we find the legends assume a different character, saints and hermits giving place to knights and ladies, and minstrels sing lays of love and pleasure in place of dwelling on the old themes of war and religion. Instead of descriptions of lives passed in deserts, and celestial visions, we have pictures of tournaments and tales of robbers, ghosts, and stirring adventures of all sorts, mingled with dreams of Eastern luxury.

Popular fury having been raised by the preaching of Peter the Hermit and others, it expended itself in the first place on those more immediately within its reach; and in Trèves the Jews were so persecuted that they frequently committed suicide, after slaying their children: multitudes of them also embraced Christianity, only to resume their real faith when the storm had passed.

In the two succeeding centuries many curious laws were enacted to suit the times,— those relating to trial by combat are among the most remarkable; we will merely instance one: If a woman of the lower classes had been violated, but the matter could not be proved, the accused man was buried up to his middle in the earth, and a stick, an ell long, put into his hand; thus he fought the woman, who was armed with a stone tied up in her veil.

Coiners were at this period boiled in kettles.

In addition to courts of law, there were now established courts of love; these were composed of select [89]women and knightly poets, who with extraordinary sagacity gave judgment in love affairs.

The service of the fair formed an essential part of knightly customs. To insult, or in any way injure a woman, was disgraceful. Woman—the ideal of beauty, gentleness, and love—inflamed each knightly bosom with a desire to deserve her favours, by deeds of valour and self-denial. She was worshipped as a protecting divinity, and knights undertook any task, however difficult, at the merest hint that it would be acceptable, even deeming themselves happy to die for her sake, and so win her approbation.

Love became an art, "a knightly study," and this submission to the gentle yoke of woman, bred in humility and religion, chiefly contributed to humanise and civilise the manners of the age; and we may thank the German element for superseding the grosser and more sensual manner in which woman was regarded previously to the rising of that nation. The historian concludes his remarks on this subject by saying, "Fidelity was the essence of true love; and such were lovers then."

In the thirteenth century arose an institution immediately allied with the neighbourhood of our river; this was the *Fehm-gerichte*, or Secret Tribunal. Engelbert, an Archbishop of Cologne, was the first president and founder of this secret court. It was in the first instance composed of a number of honourable men of every class, who joined together for the purpose of judging and punishing all evildoers; its measures [90]were chiefly directed against the licentious nobles and robber-knights; its proceedings were necessarily secret, as, were the names of the judges known, they would have been objects of vengeance to all the turbulent spirits of the day. In the fourteenth century this association numbered a hundred thousand members, all bound by a solemn oath, and known to each other by a secret sign.

No ecclesiastics, except the spiritual lord; no Jews, women, or servants, were admitted as members; nor were these amenable to the court, all accused being judged by their peers. Accusations brought before this court were only such as would not have been received by the more legal tribunals.

The accused was summoned to appear three times; and if he did not then come forward, judgment was passed on him by default, the oath of the accuser being considered sufficient proof of his guilt, and the condemned criminal was secretly and mysteriously deprived of life. His body was always found with a dagger, on which were the letters S. S. G. G.,4 plunged into it.

As an instance of the working and rude justice of this tribunal, we read the following:—

"A certain Baron Wolfgang von Cronenburg ravished a nun, and bade defiance to the laws, in his castle; but even here the arm of this secret society reached him, and he was found dead. The nun being [91] pregnant by him was released from her vows, and the possessions of her ravisher bestowed on her and her son."

An extraordinary pilgrimage was founded about the end of the thirteenth century by an Archbishop of Trèves; the pilgrims were to go to the grave of Saint Willibrod at Epternach, and there join in a general dance in her honour. During this dance the pilgrims of all ranks were linked together; first they advanced, then retired, afterwards ziz-zagging off to the right and left. This custom was kept up for many years, and is still in existence in a modified form.5

In 1473, Trèves was selected by Charles the Bold and the Emperor Frederick III. as the place where they should meet and settle the marriage of Mary of Burgundy with Maximilian, the son of Frederick; Charles was on his side to be invested with the rank of King, and receive the title of King of Burgundy.

Frederick arrived, magnificently attended; but Charles, surrounded by his nobles from the rich country of Flanders, outshone the Emperor. The latter invested Charles with the Duchy of Guelders, and a day was fixed for his coronation as King; but before the day arrived Frederick quietly took boat and dropped down the Moselle, being probably instigated by the French emissaries6 to take this step.

The disgust of Charles defrauded of a crown, and [92] of the towns-people disappointed of a spectacle, must have been excessive.

The abuses of the Romish Church now culminated, and Luther, hurling his bolt against the Roman Bishop, drove the faith of the times into two opposite extremes,— infidelity and superstition. Men's minds became unhinged; none knew what to believe; fantastic visions of every kind dazzled the eyes of all; the devil seemed to walk on earth, and men who believed in little else sought his protection. Now was the time when people believed that certain charms rendered their bodies invulnerable; and bullets, which never missed, could be cast. Gold was supposed to be obtainable by skill; and above all, the elixir of life, which should enable the possessor to lengthen his term of existence at pleasure, was eagerly sought. One charlatan asserted that gold could be extracted from Jews, and that the ashes of twenty-four of this nation would yield one ounce. In the preceding century a Bishop of Lausanne had believed in the efficacy of a spiritual anathema for driving away grasshoppers and mice, and soon after a Bishop of Coire cursed cockchafers.

The burning of witches formed one of the most remarkable features of the age of the Reformation; it had commenced at an earlier period, but became general in the sixteenth and seventeenth centuries.

In the fourteenth century the Council of Trèves condemned the belief in witches, and declared their supposed nightly expeditions to be a fabulous invention; [93] but in the fifteenth century the belief came suddenly back with fresh force, Pope Innocent VIII., in 1485, affirming the existence of witches.

Old women were more persecuted by the Lutherans than they had been by the Inquisition. They were accused of being in league with the devil, and with his help raising storms, depriving cows of milk, carrying off corn through the air, striking men and cattle dead, or afflicting them with sickness, exciting love by potions, and unnatural hate by spells.

For all these, and many other imaginary crimes, poor old women were dragged from their homes and subjected to different ordeals. Firstly, came the shaving of the head; and if any mole or scar was found, she was proclaimed a witch. Secondly, if no mole or scar, she was usually tried by either water or weight; if the former, her right thumb was tied to her left great toe, and her left thumb to her right great toe, and she was thrown into the water: if she floated, she was a witch; if weight was the test, little shrivelled-up women had no hope, for they were generally declared under weight, and tortured till they confessed. Under these tortures they confessed whatever their persecutors thought fit, and were then burned. There were many other ordeals practised in different places.

The Archbishop of Trèves, in 1589, sentenced so many women to the stake, that in two districts only two women remained. This Archbishop also condemned the Rector of the University of Trèves as a sorcerer.[24]

Towards the end of the seventeenth century, Trèves suffered much from the different armies that repeatedly traversed her territories; and in the beginning of the eighteenth century, one of its Electors had the temerity to declare war against Louis XIV., without waiting for the decision of the Empire.

Louis determined to seize on the person of the Elector, who he jeeringly named the "Little Curé of Trèves." For this purpose he despatched a regiment of Hussars from Sarre-Louis, with orders to bring him dead or alive. The Hussars endeavoured to surprise the Elector while hunting; but a certain Postmaster warned him of the plot and he fled to Ehrenbreitstein, closely followed by the Hussars. The Elector rewarded the Postmaster, by ordering that whenever he came to Ehrenbreitstein he should be allowed to eat and drink his fill of whatever he chose, that was in cellar or larder.

In 1803 the spiritual Electorates were abolished, and Trèves included in France. It now forms a portion of Rhenish Prussia.

* * *

Having touched on the leading historical events connected with Trèves, from the earliest times to the present century, we will take a survey of the city as it now exists.

Formerly Trèves occupied a large space on both sides of the Moselle, but it has in later years been confined to the right bank of the river; indeed, it cannot properly be said to be on the Moselle at all, for the principal part of the town is at some distance inland, [25] and everywhere walls shut it out from the stream, only a few detached houses appearing on the banks.

Completely modernised, Trèves yet possesses a certain look of age, owing probably to its walls with avenues of trees surrounding, and an air of decay visible throughout its streets and squares. The later style of houses are of the time of Louis XV., and many of them are good specimens of sufficiently ornamented dwellings.

The Market-place presents a most animated appearance on the great market-days; and it is with difficulty we can force our way through the crowd on those days, owing to a fashion the women have of wearing their baskets on their backs; which unwieldy things are unmercifully pushed into the ribs of the passer-by, and while he tries to recover his breath after the concussion his incautious foot probably receives a solid sabot on its tenderest part. In the Market-place stands an elegant fountain, opposite to [26] which is the Rothen Haus, formerly the town-hall: this building is now a comfortable inn, well placed for studying costumes and customs.

Within sight of the Market-place is the famous Porta Nigra; what its original use was is a matter of vague conjecture, the learned in such subjects not being able to agree in their opinions. During the middle ages it was used for ecclesiastical purposes, and was fitted up as two churches, one above the other, in which service was regularly performed: the Prussian authorities have restored it to its original state, and it is very well preserved, and is certainly quite one of the most interesting Roman buildings extant.

There are (as we stated at the commencement of this chapter) many other reminiscences of the Roman rule to be seen in Trèves, the principal of which are the bridge, the amphitheatre, and the baths: of the latter a considerable portion still remains, but of the amphitheatre only the form is left, with a mere fragment of wall at the entrance. It, in common with the other ruins in Trèves, is well kept and preserved.

The old palace of the Archbishops is now a barrack, and only interesting from its associations.

The Liebfrauen Kirche is a beautiful Gothic edifice, with noble arches of extreme lightness and delicacy of appearance; the doorway is richly carved; and, altogether, this church is as beautiful a specimen of its order of architecture as can be found.[27]

31

The Cathedral is a fine building and stands side by side with the Liebfrauen Kirche, which it far exceeds in size but to which it is inferior in beauty; it is, nevertheless, a good specimen of the Byzantine style, and from its proximity to the Liebfrauen Kirche we are able, at a glance, to contrast the different orders of architecture.

In this Cathedral is deposited the coat of our Saviour, "woven without seam from top to the bottom;" and here flocked, so lately as 1844, no less than one million one hundred thousand persons to gaze on the wonderful garment, which was exhibited to the *faithful* for eight weeks and then returned to its coffer.

There are many other churches in and around Trèves, one of which the commissionaires think very grand, and accordingly march their slaves, the sight-seers, off to visit it, and expect them to fall into raptures with a whitewashed, high-roofed ball-room, covered with tawdry, coarsely-painted arabesques, and indifferent pictures; the slaves generally gratify their tyrants by falling into unbounded raptures, and nearly twist their necks off to get a look at the paintings on the ceiling: latterly, little looking-glasses have been provided, to save them from getting cricks in their necks.

About six miles from Trèves, on the Luxembourg road, is a village called Igel. Here is preserved a very curious stone obelisk, covered with carvings of figures and inscriptions: as usual, there is a considerable [98]dispute as to its origin and purpose, but it undoubtedly is a very curious relic of bygone days, and is not without beauty in design and execution.

Luxembourg is a very strong place, so scientifically fortified that it is most difficult for an uninitiated person to find his way into it; and having done so, the town is so wretchedly stupid and dull that the visitor generally comes to the conclusion that he has taken a good deal of trouble for nothing, and hastens to make his way out: which task he finds not less difficult than the entry. From the walls very striking views might be seen, only the sentries order you off immediately, especially if you have so deadly an implement as a sketch-book in your hand; however, we have no particular cause to expatiate on Luxembourg, as it is only one small feeder of our river.

Roman Monument in Igel.

[99]

1The foundation of this legend is, that portions of canals have been found between Trèves and Cologne, but it is supposed they were separate canals, not portions of one large one; therefore, perhaps, the duck did not swim all the way from Trèves.

2Cathedral.

3Grimm supposes Eigel and Orendel to be Ulysses and Laertes.

4Stock (stick), Stein (stone), Gras (grass), Grun (green).

5As the author was informed at Trèves.

6*Query*, Was this the origin of taking French leave?

[Contents]

CHAPTER VII.

Ferry.

That portion of our river which lies between Trèves and Coblence is the most beautiful, and the part usually visited by the few who allow themselves the enjoyment of seeing scenery yet unspoiled by Art. The Moselle at this present time is much what the Rhine was half a century ago. No great roads line the banks, cutting off the quaint houses of the old towns and villages from the river-side; and the towns and villages themselves are, with some few exceptions, far more picturesque than those on the Rhine. Their old water-towers and walls still lave their bases in the stream, as those of St. Goarshausen-on-Rhine did until a few years back, when the new road drove them inland.

In places where the rocks approach closely to the [100]river, the usual arrangement of the houses is in one long street, with behind it ruined towers perched at intervals upon the ascending walls, which straggle through the vineyards, till the rise becomes too sudden for them to climb or intruders to pass over. Where the space is larger, the houses are clustered among walnut-trees, which grow to an immense size. Perhaps the greatest charm of all in descending our river is the absence of those swarms of mere sight-seers who infest the Rhine,—the trifling discomforts of a more unfrequented route being sufficient to deter these garrulous butterflies from "doing" the Moselle; and as yet Murray has not given in detail the number of turrets to each castle on this river, for eager watchers to "tell off" as the steamer breasts the stream. Still it is remarkable how few of all those that pass the mouth of the Moselle at Coblence ascend its waters.

We now invite those who cannot in person see "the blue Moselle" to embark their minds in our skiff, and as we glide along we will tell them tales of the old time, when the ruined towers above our heads clanged with the tramp of armed men, and echoed to songs of love and wine.

Trèves and its bridge are shut out by the trees, and the river nymphs surround us with garlands and with song.

Now our boat adown the stream
Floats, as in a happy dream,—
Thoughts to fancy's kingdom go,
There, like waters, tranquil flow;
[101]
Airy palaces they build
Where our kindred spirits dwell,
Who with woven sunbeams gild
Regions that we love so well.

Rippling now the gentle waves
(Gay sunshine our pathway paves),
Sing to us as on we glide
Down the swiftly-glancing tide:
"Happiness and harmless mirth
Innocently we enjoy,
So the denizens of earth
May, like us, their time employ,—
Working we sing,
In leisure hours we play;
O'er toil we fling
A garland ever gay."

O'er our heads the dark rocks rise,
Stern their mass the stream defies,—
Round their base the dark wave flows,
Battling, silently, she goes:
Thus in life, too frequent, rocks
Stand before us in our way;
And their bulk our passage blocks,
Bidding us our course to stay.
Shall we at their bidding turn,
Fearful of their aspect stern?
No: for patiently we may
Round, or through them, win our way.

The little incidents seen on the banks of the river as we move along are eminently picturesque, and give life and reality to what we should otherwise almost [102]imagine to be a dream of beauty, rather than real actual scenes, where toil and labour are at work. Such foregrounds, too, for artists! Here is a woman mowing: further down, one impels a heavy boat along by means of a pole: there red cows stand, half in the water, half on a grassy slope, with the reflected green of which their red contrasts. Again, as we approach a village, some of the maidens are seen drawing water; while others, in groups and attitudes that present endless studies, wash their gay clothing, or bleach long strips of brownish linen.

33

Boat-building is carried on at nearly every village, and the smoke from the accompanying fire wreathes among the walnut-trees. In reality, the people work hard; but it is difficult to divest our minds of the idea that they are merely sauntering about, and forming groups for their own amusement and the delight of others. All is so complete in loveliness, that it seems unreal.[103]

The ribs of the great flat-bottomed boats look like skeletons of some curious animal, which the apparent loungers are examining at their ease; and the nearly completed barge seems to be a sort of summer-house, in which the idler can sit, or under which he may smoke his pipe in the shade,—for, of course, all smoke. Usually the long stem with the earthenware or china bowl is the medium by which the fragrant weed is inhaled, but sometimes a few inches of coarse stick (in appearance) is the substitute.

Boat-building.

These boats, when finished, are used for all sorts of purposes. The want of good roads, and the fact of the stream being less rapid than that of the Rhine, as well as the absence of steam-tugs, makes the Moselle more lively with barges and small boats, especially the latter; though, of course, there being only three or four steamers on the whole distance (about 150 miles) between Trèves and Coblence, the absence of those [104] puffing drawbacks to tranquil enjoyment renders the Moselle more quiet on the whole.

The larger barges carry iron, earthenware, charcoal, bark, wine, and general cargoes; while the smaller ones are filled with market produce of all sorts going to be sold in the larger towns, and numbers of these small boats are kept at each village for the residents to cross to their farms or vineyards on the opposite bank. There are also ferry-boats, large enough for carts and oxen, or horses, at nearly every cluster of houses.

Boat-building.

Often watching these great boats with their miscellaneous lading, or waiting our own turn to cross, we have been struck by the contrast between the young fair children with flaxen hair and the careworn countenances of the parents, whose skin is nearly as brown as that of a Maltese boatman, his approaching to claret-colour. The peasantry are, as far as we could judge or learn, a simple, contented race, working hard, and in bad seasons ill-fed.[105]

THE FERRY.

On grassy bank the village stands,
The crowds returning, throng
The ferry-boat, which quickly lands,
Impelled by arms so strong.
The heavy boat is filled with men,
With women, and with carts;
Amongst the crowd the children
Move with their lightsome hearts.
The women's brows are stamped with care,
The men with toil are worn;
But midst them stand those children fair,
Those happy newly-born.
The doom of man, "for life to toil,"
Rests on the parents both,
But on that young, fresh, virgin soil,
Even the Sun is loth.
His hot red hand too fierce to press,
Where innocence and love
Call for a mother's sweet caress
And from the sky above
Speak unto us, who labour here,
This message through them sent:
"Live, love, and worship, in God's fear;
"To labour be content;

34

"So shall ye live, and dying, shall not miss
"The life immortal, in the realms of bliss!"

The different seasons of the year, of course, bring different incidents on our river into existence, each in its proper turn. The hay-harvest is a very lively time [106] upon its banks; everywhere the green slopes are rid of their superfluous load, and boats cross and recross the river with the sweet-scented cargoes, some of which are stored, some transferred to larger bottoms for transportation down the stream.

Later comes the corn-harvest, then the boats are freighted with the golden ears; soon after an equally busy time sets in, when every sort of boat is seen piled with small branches of the oak: the leaves are stripped from the branches so brought home, and, being carefully dried, they form an excellent material with which the people stuff their mattresses, this making, as they assert, much warmer and softer beds, than straw. Every village possesses a right of cutting bedding at [107] some place, and the different inhabitants have days allotted them by the authorities, on which they may help themselves.

The winter draws near and the vintage sets in, then all boats are employed on this absorbing service; the little boats, with large casks on board, look in the distance very much like gondolas: wherever the eye rests, nothing is seen that has not some connexion with the great event of the year on the Moselle. However, the vintage has a chapter to itself, so we will not dwell upon it here.

Carrying firewood is the last great occupation of the year for the smaller boats, and it is well for those who can procure a good supply of fuel, for the winter is cold and severe; unfortunately, too, wood is very scarce and dear, and though somewhat cheaper on the Moselle than in most parts of Germany, yet a good fire is quite out of the reach of the poorer classes, and they scrape together every morsel to enable them to feed the iron stoves which warm their cottages. [108]

The river is in parts so shallow that breakwaters are built out from the banks, in order to deepen the centre of the stream; this, of course, makes the water run swifter, and it requires great toil of many horses to tug the barges up the stream. Floating down these rapids is agreeable enough, and the descent is made with very little labour, towns and villages succeeding each other on the banks, the approaches to them being lined with fruit-trees, of which the walnut and cherry are the most conspicuous.

The cherries are excellent, and so plentiful that children will often refuse a handful when offered, having previously gorged themselves at home. Numbers are exported, going by river to Coblence, and so on down the Rhine.

Apricots are also abundant in good seasons. They are grown on standard trees.

Garden produce of all sorts abounds, and apples and pears drop unheeded to the ground.

Through incidents like these, on bank and river, we glide on. We have, perhaps, halted during the midday heat at some inviting spot, where the cool shadows reposed beneath the walnuts; now the evening draws near, and rounding a corner, our resting-place for the night appears. The thin mist rising from the river obscures the base of the church, whose sharply-pointed spire is conspicuous above the trees; lights fall in tremulous lines from the high windows, and in the air is the sound of— [109]

CHURCH MUSIC.

From the church the anthem pealing,
O'er the wave is gently stealing:
Now it swells, now dies away,
Making holy harmony.
The spire from out the trees
Our eyes directs on high;
The sounds which swell the breeze,
The heavens to us bring nigh;
For while we listen to the song

35

Of glory rais'd to "Him on high,"
Our thoughts soar up, and dwell among
Those realms where Immortality,
In angel forms and bright array,
Before God's throne for ever pray,
And Hallelujahs joyous raise
To their "Almighty Maker's" praise.

[110]
[Contents]

CHAPTER VIII.

Piesport.

From Trèves to Trittenheim the scenery of our river, although very pleasing, has not yet attained to its full beauty; the Moselle, woman as she has become, [111] is still scarcely matured in beauty; many charms are hers already, but until approaching Neumagen her life does not reach the fulness of her summer glory. Then, indeed, the full enchantment of her beauty breaks upon us, as, often in life, we have been in the habit of seeing a lovely girl pass from childhood into the graces of early womanhood, we admire and love; but at some future day we suddenly perceive that the lovely girl has become a glorious woman, replete with every grace. The change seems to take place in a day, even in an hour: some incident, trifling perchance in itself, has awoke the spirit, and the lately shy and timid girl has become a woman in spirit as in name; losing none of the happy loveliness of her earlier years, she has acquired a dignity and nameless, indefinable grace, which completes her beauty and robs us of our hearts.

Such has our Moselle become when she winds among the mountains past Neumagen and Piesport.

The promontory at the back of Neumagen is divided into two parts by the little river Drohn. It is supposed by many that it was on the bank of this little stream that the celebrated Palace of the Thirty Towers stood. This palace, built by the Archbishop Nicetius of Trèves, is supposed to have been most beautiful, and formed entirely of marble, with pleasure-grounds sloping to the stream and river. The description given of these gardens by the poet, Venantius Fortunatus, reads more like an Eastern account of those gardens of Paradise sometimes for [112] a moment unveiled to the wanderer in the Arabian desert. Bishofstein (lower down the stream) also claims the honour of being on the site of the Palace of the Thirty Towers, but it does not in any way answer the description. Whether the banks of the Drohn were the site of this marble palace or not, the beauty of the situation certainly gives it a claim to have been so, and the Archbishops did possess a country-house near Neumagen.

A few miles below Trèves we pass Pfalzel, which lies on the left bank; this little town is interesting, as it is said to be the site of the beautiful legend of Genoveva, handed down to us in so many different versions.

[Contents]

LEGEND OF GENOVEVA.

The Pfalz-graf Siegfried was married to a lovely and virtuous lady, named Genoveva, and they lived together in great happiness and content, until a wicked courtier, named Golo, whose attentions the lady had repulsed, plotted how he might ruin her in her lord's esteem.

To this end he poisoned the Pfalz-graf's mind against his virtuous wife, and so, deeming her guilty of crimes she never even imagined, her lord drove Genoveva from his castle, that so she might be slain of wild beasts or die of hunger.

Genoveva, as she passed out from the castle gates, threw her wedding-ring into the water, that so the [113] crime of her lord might be lessened, as he was thus released from the marriage-tie.

Time passed on, and Siegfried, being on a hunting excursion, wished for food and rest; he therefore ordered a tent to be pitched on the banks of a stream. No sooner was this done than two fishermen arrived with a great fish, which they presented to the Pfalz-graf;

36

the fish being opened, a ring was found, which the Pfalz-graf no sooner saw than he perceived it was that of his dead wife.

Returning home he was much troubled at this circumstance, and falling asleep he dreamt that he saw a dragon persecuting Genoveva, who still was dearer to him than all the world beside. He related this dream to Golo, who pacified him for a time: but again he dreamt, and in his dream he hunted a pure white hind, following, and persecuting it remorselessly; awaking, he felt that the hind was Genoveva, and he was indeed a cruel huntsman, who had chased a spotless deer to death.

He ordered everything to be prepared for the chase,—why, he knew not, but felt the dream must be followed out; Golo was seized with agony when the Pfalz-graf set forth, and secretly followed his master's steps.

A spotless hind was found, and the Pfalz-graf eagerly followed on her track, wounding her with an arrow; on sped the hind, until, with a last bound, it forced its way through the bushes, and fell bleeding and exhausted at Genoveva's feet.[114]

Siegfried followed close, and threw himself on his knees before his injured wife, who had been wonderfully preserved from death, and, together with the child to which she had given birth, nourished by the poor deer, which now was dying of her wounds.

Pointing to her babe, Genoveva showed that in every feature it was the counterpart of her lord: thus was Golo's treachery made manifest, and his head, being struck from off the body, was exposed upon the castle walls.

Another legend of Pfalzel tells of a wicked nun, who, by the devil's aid, worked a magic garment and presented it to the Archbishop; immediately on putting it on horrible desires seized on him, and he felt as if the fiend were dragging him to perdition. Throwing it off, others tried it, and on all it had the same effect; being therefore convinced of the iniquity of the worker, the Archbishop turned the nun out of the convent, but finding that her sister nuns were as bad as she, he was compelled to treat them all in a similar manner: the garment, however, still exists, and is worn by many.

Inland of Pfalzel is Rammstein, where a certain Count of Vianden (like Adalbert of St. Cross) came to an untimely end by an overfondness for wine. He had once taken the Bishop prisoner and put him into fetters; this latter never forgot or forgave, so, knowing the Count's fondness for wine, he, one very sultry day, sent a string of carts filled with [115]barrels past the walls of the Count's strong castle; down swooped the Count's followers, like beasts of prey as they were, and carried off the convoy; then they all set to work drinking, in the true German fashion.

While thus carousing, the armed followers of the Bishop suddenly surprised them, and the castle was taken and burnt; the Bishop shouted to the Count, who in his turn was put in fetters, "Behold the consequence of raising thy hand against the Lord's anointed!"

Near Pfalzel several brooks run into the Moselle; one on the same bank, named the Kill, passes Rammstein, and flowing through a charming valley, waters a large strip of most productive garden-ground, which extends from the Moselle to some distance inland.

These lateral valleys are very frequent on our river. We can scarcely wander along her banks for a quarter of a mile but a recess in the neighbouring hills is seen, through which a little stream comes dancing. Penetrating into the gorge we find busy little mills at work, and are led into scenery which at every turn seems to increase in beauty. We shall hereafter have to describe some of these lateral valleys, so need not now dwell on their delights.

On the opposite shore, which is watered by another stream, is Grünhaus, and above it Grüneberg. From these vineyards come the most highly-prized wines of the Moselle, though many think the wines of Zeltingen more delicate in flavour.[116]

Past little islands, and through rich fields filled with garden produce, we glide on, following the serpentine course of our river. The wood-embosomed villages peep at us as we go by, each group of houses has its church rising in the midst: gradually the banks grow steeper, hills swell up inland, and here and there come down to look on the Moselle. These reconnoiterers retire, and having told their chiefs of the approach of the glorious stream, at

Trittenheim we find the right bank covered with mountain-giants, come to do homage to the spirit of the waters.

At Trittenheim is one of those flying bridges, almost peculiar to the Moselle. It is thus formed: two strong towers are built, one on each side of the stream; from the summits of these towers, attached to great posts built into the solid wall, stretches a rope, which falls in a curve over the river; a stout cord attached to a swivel, which runs freely along the rope, descends to the surface of the river, and to it is fastened a barge, which propelled by the action of the swift running stream, and guided by the boatman, passes from side to side at his pleasure, carrying heavy loads, with little labour to the ferryman.

Where the breadth of the river admits, these sort of flying bridges are used; in other parts, those with which the reader is probably familiar on the Rhine are in operation; and again, where the stream is sluggish, barges unattached to any rope are poled up stream, and floated across.

Trittenheim was the birth-place of the celebrated |117|Trithemius, famous for his many writings and his learning. He, in common with all learned men of his time (end of fifteenth century), was considered a sorcerer, and the Emperor Maximilian applied to him to raise the spirit of his deceased wife, Mary of Burgundy. This he is said to have done, and the dead Princess reappeared in all the charms of her youthful beauty: but a more probable account of this transaction is given in the following version, taken from the beautiful poem in the *Mosel sagen.*

TRITHEMIUS AND THE EMPEROR.

One very dark night a man wrapped in a mantle, so as to conceal his features, entered the cloister at Spanheim, and demanded to see the Abbot.

Trithemius (the Abbot) advanced to meet his visitor, who he immediately recognised as the Emperor Maximilian. The Emperor requested him to raise the shade of his first wife, Mary; upon which Trithemius took him by the hand, and leading him out of doors, pointed to two bright constellations in the form of staves, which were shining in the sky, and addressed him as follows:—

"You see there, my Prince, the two principles of government; by ruling with the one, bad princes beat down their subjects beneath their feet, and cause those little stars, which represent drops of blood and tears, to flow; in that garden where the seeds of time are ripening, this staff will stand like a |118|parched trunk, but the other staff will flourish green as a palm-tree, unhurt by the heat of the summer's day; for this last is a righteous sceptre, a staff of pure gold, serving to support and strengthen those who lean trustfully upon it, and use it to benefit their subjects. Choose, then, O Monarch, with which staff thou wilt rule."

While the Priest thus spoke another star shone forth, and directing the Emperor's attention towards it, Trithemius again addressed him.

"I see, O King, a young and smiling face beam from the newly-risen star. Tearless and blissfully it smiles on you, wearing the look of your glorified wife. Pain and tears are left behind her in the grave, on which they blossom like pale roses. Mary beckons to you from on high to join her in the gardens of God.

"Choose, then, thy sceptre, O Prince. Erect to thy loved wife a monument of deeds. To act is a ruler's duty. We priests *have* had bestowed upon us a magic virtue; it consists in wiping away your tears, and animating you to tread the right path with the sceptre of blessings in your hand.

"Be strong, be wise, my Prince, and receive my blessing on your noble path. Farewell."

The Prince, perceiving the value of the counsel he had received, departed through the night, which now was luminous, with the words of truth.

The promontory on which Trittenheim is situated |119|is clothed with fruit-trees, and rivals in fertility the opposite shore, on which, a little lower down, Neumagen is situated.

Before reaching Neumagen we pass a little chapel, erected at the spot where, according to tradition, the waters of the Moselle ceased to be tinged with the blood shed at Trèves in the massacre of Christian martyrs.

Neumagen enjoys a most agreeable site. Sheltered by the hills which rise at its back, it faces the bold cliffs that now have arisen on the left bank of our river. On ascending the hills at the back of the town we find ourselves on a level platform, with the Moselle on one side of us and the Drohn on the other; beyond these, other table-lands swell into hills, and varied outlines of distant mountains curve into the sky.

On this elevated table-land a refreshing breeze blows, even on the most sultry days, and the tender blue lines of the receding hills give an air of coolness which is delicious to the heated pedestrian. Such variety of scenery as the walking tourist meets on the Moselle is scarcely to be exceeded; hill and dale, mountain, river, wood, and plain, all are there combining their charms.

It was over these hills that Constantine was marching when, at break of day,1 the fiery cross appeared in the sky, with the inscription, "*In hoc vince.*" Wonder arose in the minds of Constantine and his [120]legions, but none could interpret the meaning of the celestial sign. At night, in a dream, Constantine saw Jesus with a cross in his arms, like to that he had seen in the heavens; and the vision commanded him to attach a mark of the same form to his standard, telling him that by so doing he should vanquish all his enemies.

Arriving at Trèves, Constantine, mindful of his dream and the celestial sign, called together cunning artificers; and a cross, surmounted with a crown of gold and jewels, was set upon the lance from which the purple standard of royalty floated.

And all his enemies were conquered, in accordance with the words spoken to him in his dream. So Christianity triumphed over idolatry.

* * *

Walking across the promontory that lies between Neumagen and Piesport, we found the ground covered with the delicate autumn crocus, whose jewels sparkled among the grass; and apples, with their ruddy hues, lay beneath the trees, from which they had abundantly fallen.

Piesport is confined by the mountain at its back to one narrow, straggling street; it possesses a handsome church, from which we saw, soon after our arrival, issue forth a long procession. First came men, two and two, clad in blue frocks; then children, followed by women in like order; these preceded the old priest and choristers; then again came men; and, lastly, old women. The procession wound its chanting stream along, round the little town, and returning, made the [121]circuit of the church and re-entered the edifice. The object of the ceremony was to charm rain from the sky by their chanting. The performers and assisters ill the scene gossiped and chatted to each other in the intervals of singing, and the poor old priest seemed quite wearied, and glad to return to his church. The singing did not in any way influence the weather, certainly for some weeks.

The mountain behind Piesport is entirely covered with vineyards. These celebrated vineyards were considered the best on the Moselle in the earlier part of last century; but having gained this reputation for their wine, the cultivators introduced a worse sort of grape, which bore more fruit, in order to make a greater quantity of wine; but, fortunately for the place, a new Curé, who was appointed in 1770, induced them to restore the old sort of vine, and thus regain the reputation they were rapidly losing.

Having succeeded in getting up nearly to the summit of the mountain without *un coup de soleil*, we got among groves of picturesquely-formed oak, many of the trees being of considerable size. Throwing ourselves down beneath their grateful shade, a fine view of the surrounding district is before us. This view we have endeavoured to lay before our readers in the vignette at the head of the chapter. The spire of the church at Piesport is seen cutting against the bed of the river, and the peep of distance gives a good idea of the peculiar formation of the hills.

The hills of the Moselle are not hills in the ordinary [122]acceptation of the word, as they all form part of a high table-land, which extends from near here to beyond Andernach-on-Rhine, on the left bank, and on the right to Bingen. The range on the right bank are called the Hunsruck mountains; that on the left bank, the Eifel. Through the great table-land thus formed flow the Rhine and Moselle; thus the banks of both rivers are very similar in formation, and average about the same height: but the Moselle, being a much smaller river, of course her banks appear more mountainous; the ranges also approach nearer to the stream, and the lateral valleys are far more frequent.

It is astonishing at first, after climbing unceasingly for an hour, to find one's self standing on a gently undulating plain waving with grain, and forest-trees growing in masses. The river is then seen to be in a gorge, worn by the perpetual action of her waters, and we have only attained to the natural level of the country.

This level is, however, broken by many other gorges, each containing its stream, bounding downwards to our river. Towards the horizon also (as we have mentioned in describing the view above Neumagen) the table-land generally rises into higher ranges; thus there is never any monotony about the scenery, which is enlivened by the spires of churches, and busy labourers at work in what seemed to us like Jack and the Bean-stalk's country. It so strongly resembles the description given, where the immortal Jack climbs up and up his bean-stalk, until at length he arrives at the level of a new world.[123]

In autumn, when the weeds, &c. are being burnt, the scenes on this table-land are very striking. Far as the eye can reach wreathe up the columns of white smoke, spreading a purifying smell of burning, and wrapping the view in a filmy veil that increases its beauty.

The name of Piesport is derived from Pipini Portus, the place having been thus called from being an *allod* of the Carlovingian house, of which Pepin was the founder.

Clausen, which lies at a short distance from Piesport, contains a miraculous picture of the Virgin, which was originally brought from Trèves by the zealous Saint Eberhard, whose hermitage stood in the forest.

The Saint built a chapel, and in it he placed this wonderful picture: here many miracles were performed; on one occasion a paralytic man was completely restored to the use of his limbs: he threw away his crutches, and walked home, no longer requiring the horse that had brought him.

The miracles wrought in the Saint's little chapel gave great offence to the constituted Priest of Clausen, and eventually the picture was removed to his church; but it ceased to perform miracles, its virtue was gone, and now it is only regarded with veneration on account of its former celebrity.

Having now arrived in the heart of the wine-district, we will proceed to give some little account of the vintage, which occupies all attention and employs all hands in these parts.[124]

And, with the merry peasants, we will sing the praise of their good genius:—

THE VINE.
The vine! the vine!
Hurrah for the vine!
That gives us wine—
Bright, joyous wine;
Hurrah for the merry vine!
O maiden mine,
Press out the wine
With feet that shine
Like gems in mine,—
Press out the glorious wine!
The clusters press
With firm caress
Of glist'ning feet,
That merry meet:
Flow freely forth, O wine!
Then, maiden sweet,
With full lip meet
My offer'd kiss;
Complete my bliss,
And quaff with me the wine.

So love and wine
Shall thus combine,
And no alloy
Shall mar our joy,
As thus we quaff the wine.
So, sing the vine—
Hurrah for the vine!
That gives us wine—
Bright, joyous wine;
Hurrah for the merry vine!

[123]

1 According to Eusebius.
[Contents]

CHAPTER IX.

On the Moselle the vintage is still conducted in the old-fashioned way, much of the wine being still pressed from the bunches by the feet. The clusters, which have been carefully cut from the trees, are placed in the baskets (which the people seem always to wear on their backs), and [126] borne down the hill-side to the village, where they are tumbled into great tubs, in which they are crushed, if not by the feet, by wooden mallets.

The long toil of carrying up great basketsful of dressing for the roots, of hacking round the vines, of carefully tying up the boughs and tending them in every possible way, repairing the walls and steps, and placing beneath the fruit-bunches flat stones to refract the heat on to their lower sides, is ended; all having prospered, joy is at its height, for plenty will fill the homes of the cultivators during the coming winter.

The peasantry suffer great hardships in bad years; and, unfortunately, these more frequently recur than good.

Having, week after week, toiled up and down the nearly perpendicular cliffs, and worked amid their vineyards unmindful alike of sun and rain, it is very sad to think that generally the gain is small for so much labour; and even in good years, although the peasantry benefit considerably, yet it is not they, but the wine-buyers, who make the principal profit.

In every village may be seen one or two houses, evidently occupied by a class far above the peasantry. To these houses are attached large cellars, through whose open doors we sometimes see great casks piled up; the owners of these dwellings are small merchants, who buy up the grapes from the poorer people, paying by the weight. They are the real gainers by a good year, for they rule the prices of the market; and by advancing sums when necessary [127] to the peasants, the latter are in a measure bound to accommodate them. That all do benefit is, however, an undoubted fact; and the happy vintage-time is the most joyful season of the year upon our river's banks.

THE HARVEST.
The green leaves wither with the autumn's breath;
The brown leaves falling, pass from life to death.
The winter, stealing on with silent feet,
Hastens the yearly cycle to complete.
But on our river's banks no sorrows dwell,
No sigh is breath'd for summer on Moselle;
For autumn's glory throws its ripening beam
Upon the cluster'd vine, whose branches teem
With the rich fulness of the luscious prize,
Which each year gives to man, ere yet it dies.
The evening spreads its shadow over earth,
From ev'ry vineyard comes the sound of mirth;
High spring the fiery rockets into air,

And hearty shouts the vintage-time declare.
The ruddy fires illumine ev'ry hill,
Reports of arms the throbbing valleys fill;[128]
These from the river back are lustrous thrown,
Those by the rocks repeated thunder on.
Thus is the grape-god welcom'd to his throne.
And Bacchus rules, in vintage-time, alone.

With sounds like these the great harvest of the year is ushered in. Rejoicing and merriment rule all hearts; the voice breaks forth in song, and the dance is followed by unwearied feet. Every thought for months past has been directed to the vine. Other harvests have been stored, with thankfulness, but the vintage has ever been *the* great subject of conversation in every cottage and at every well. The tedious watches are at an end, for, thickly clustered on every tree, the grapes are ready for the gatherer's hand.

Our river is now more beautiful than ever: the panorama at our feet is gorgeous with crimson and gold; groups of children pile the grapes into the baskets; boats, laden with the rich treasure, are passing to and fro; and from them we hear the voices of the rowers, which, re-echoing from the rocks, roll away into distance, filling the great valley with songs of happiness:—

From the Mosel's clust'ring hills
Freely flows the sparkling wine;
Midst them cooling water-rills,
Through the greenwoods pleasant shine.
These sweet draughts of beauty give
To the charmèd eyes of men;
Let us hasten, then, and live
With woods and rivulets again;[129]
Our eyes shall feast on streams, our lips on wine;
We'll quaff by night—by day we'll garlands twine.
And with these garlands gay
The lovely maids we'll crown;
So joyous pass the day—
The night in goblets drown:
Life thus shall roll its days and nights along,
We'll pass the hours away with cup and song.

The whole course of the Moselle is more or less sheeted with vineyards. Wherever a shelf of rock is accessible, or can be made so, there are the vines. Within the old walls of the mouldering castles are vineyards; upon the nearly level ground are fields of vines; hanging from every wall, and climbing round every window, are the rich green leaves and graceful tendrils of this wine-giving plant. And yet there is no sameness; from the peculiar formation of the hills there is always some outjutting crag or overhanging precipice, with roof of trees, to break the lines of the vineyards. Great masses of forest still remain in many places, reserved for fire-wood and other purposes: the vineyards, too, are for the most part formed of old vines; their foliage, consequently, is more luxuriant. Owing to these reasons the vine does not assume on the Moselle that monotonous appearance that it presents in many parts of the Rhine, and generally in France. Interspersed with the vines are numbers of wild flowers, of which the white convolvulus is the most conspicuous; its graceful flower contrasts beautifully with the deep rich green of the supporting [130] plant, and where the vines festoon, wreaths of unsurpassed loveliness are formed.

Piesport is considered the centre of the wine district, and its wine bears a high reputation, though other names bear a higher price, and a few of the wines are better flavoured. Almost all the Moselle wine is white, and has a scented flavour and exquisite *bouquet*; it is thought by many superior to Rhine wine, but it will not bear transport so well.

Even the most ordinary table-wine has generally a sparkling freshness, most grateful to the drinker, as it assuages his thirst much better than other wines; but what we term "sparkling Moselle" is only to be obtained in Trèves or Coblence, and even then it is not like our idea of that wine: therefore it must, like port and sherry, be prepared expressly to suit English palates.

Some of the red wine is tolerable, but not to be compared to the red wines of the Rhine and the Ahr valley; it has something of the roughness of the latter, but not its flavour.

They have in many places in Germany what is termed the "Grape Cure." The season for this begins as soon as the grapes are ripe enough to be eaten; and the cure consists simply in munching as many bunches as the patient can possibly swallow,—about fourteen pounds being considered a fair day's eating for one person: nothing else is to be taken. Whether this cramming cures the patient of anything but love for grapes is doubtful; but it must have that effect, so it is perhaps properly called "Grape Cure." [131]

Little paths lead up to the hill-sides through the vineyards. Often steps in the solid rock have had to be cut, and the labour and perseverance must have been immense. When the vintage approaches, these paths are closed by great bundles of thorn, and other signs and marks are put up to warn off intruders.

In bad years more vinegar is made than wine; often even they do not attempt to make the latter.

The completion of the vintage is celebrated as it began, by firing and shouting, dancing and singing, and then the toil of tending the vines recommences; but if the season has been propitious, the result may be easily read in the features of the peasants, which are now for a time released from the anxious contracted look they wore through the summer and earlier part of the autumn.

So much in celebration of wine; but, ever mindful of our beautiful Moselle, we will close this vintage chapter, with its praise of wine, with a few lines in praise of water, and thus preserve that happy balance between the two fluids which is the true secret of enjoyment. Both are good; both are gifts to be rightly used and thankfully enjoyed: but if the palm is to be given to one over the other, it should not be to the usurper Wine, who generally sits upon his sister's throne.

PRAISE OF WATER.
Many sing in praise of Wine,
Many toast the bounteous Vine;
But I will sing in praise of Water,
Earth's fairest, best, and sweetest daughter.
[132]
Many love the grape to sip,
Carrying goblets to the lip;
But I will rather seek the spring,
Its pure delights will rather sing.
Wine will cheer, but also steep
Senses in a troubled sleep;
Water ever thirst assuages,
Cooling us when fever rages.
Wine, like man its maker, flows,
Joy mixt up with many woes;
So water, made by "Him above,"
For ever flows a stream of love.

[133]
[Contents]

CHAPTER X.

Veldenz.

A little below Piesport the course of our river is obstructed by a huge mass of nearly perpendicular rock, descending so abruptly into the water, that no [134] path can be made round its base. From the top of this tremendous rock the best view on the whole river is obtained. From there the eye can follow the windings of the stream as it serpentines through the hills, for many miles.

Unable to force her way through, the river bends off to the right, and wins by concession what she cannot gain by force, affording a lesson to her sex; teaching them to encircle by affection, instead of battling against the rock. By the latter course she *may* at length succeed in her desires, but not without fretting and chafing the hard rock, causing many a line upon its once smooth brow; and, finally, when the way is worn, the passage forced, will not the sullen rock for ever hang, darkening with its shadow the stream conqueror, and threatening to fall and overwhelm the persevering brawler? while, by the course here taken, the glad wave circles with her bright arms the lordly rock, and the sunlight on his face is reflected in her bosom; while the light from her gay, happy breast, is thrown back upon his manly front.

At this corner, too, the tree-groups teach us the same lesson; repeated and beautified by the tender water hues, they, in lending beauty to the stream, enhance their own, and give another of the innumerable instances in which by nature we are shown how all things are adapted and suited to their several stations; and, by aiding and assisting one another, increase their own beauty or usefulness: thus should it be in life.[135]

REFLECTIONS.

The dark shades quiver
Where the tree-tops bend
Over the river,
To whose depths they lend
Their leafy beauty, which reflected lies
Within the wave, like love that never dies;
But ever from the loved one back is thrown,
Encircling him whose love is all her own.

* * *

On the promontory which we are now leaving behind us on the right are several little villages, of which Emmel is the principal. It is celebrated for a schism which took place there.

In 1790, the Directory at Paris wished the Curé of Emmel to take the same oath they had compelled the French clergy to pronounce; and on receiving the Curé's refusal, he was proscribed. All his flock accompanied the Curé on his being driven forth, until he thus addressed them: "I quit you, but my spirit will always remain with you. At Bornhofen, whither I now go, I shall say the mass every morning at nine, and you can in spirit join in the service."

They all promised so to do; and every day at nine the people collected in the church, and said their prayers without a Curé.

After some years the Curé died, and a new one was appointed, but the people of Emmel persisted in saying their prayers by themselves without any assistance; and, in spite of all remonstrances, many families remained [136] schismatics until a few years back. It is doubtful whether they have all returned to their former allegiance, even at the present time.

Round the pebbly bed in which our river sings along her course where her banks widen, then again beneath impending cliffs, we hurry on, past Minnheim, Rondel, Winterich, and other little nests of vitality, from which the labourers come forth to cultivate the fertile soil.

Two pretty legends are told of this district; the first is called "The Cell of Eberhard;" the second, "The Blooming Roses;" and there is an evident connexion between the two.

[Contents]

THE CELL OF EBERHARD.

A mother, being provoked, said to her unoffending child, "Go off to the devil!" The poor girl, frightened, wandered into the woods, then covered with snow.

Soon the mother, growing calm, became anxious about her child, and sought her everywhere, but she could not be found: lamenting, she wept all night.

At daybreak she arose, and induced her neighbours to join her in her search; but no tracks were found in the freshly-fallen snow.

The mother then sought Eberhard's Cell, and wept and prayed till four days and nights had passed. She now requested the priest to say a mass for her lost child. No sooner

44

had the priest raised the Host on [137]high, than a tender voice sounding from the forest said, "Your little girl yet lives."

Out sprang the mother, and there, beneath the trees, she found her little daughter, a nosegay of summer flowers in one hand and a green twig in the other. With tears of joy the mother clasped her, and asked her how she had been preserved.

"Dear mother," replied the child, "has always been with me. Dear mother carried a light, and with her ran a little dog, white as the snow, and *so* faithful and kind."

Then the mother perceived that the Virgin had guarded her child; and she led the little girl into Eberhard's Cell, where they offered the wreath at the Virgin's shrine.

Still blossoms the wreath, embalmed by love and thankful prayer.

[Contents]

THE BLOOMING ROSES.

Within the forest stood a little chapel, in which was a statue of the Virgin. Hither came a young girl, and day by day adorned it with fresh flowers. From the Madonna's arms the infant Jesus smiled upon the child. Thus passed the spring and summer. The girl, devoted to her occupation, and her heart filled with love for Jesus, thought less and less upon the things of this world. One thought alone troubled her as the autumn advanced; this was, that in winter she would not be able to find flowers to adorn the chapel.[138]

This sad thought weighed heavily on her till one day, when sitting weaving a rose-wreath for the child Jesus, a voice said in her ear, "Be not faint-hearted: are not the summer's blessings still present with thee? let the present be sufficient for thee:" and so the girl wove on with lightened heart.

When winter came and the roses faded, the young girl was lying on her death-bed; her only sorrow was leaving the Virgin and child Jesus so lonely in the forest.

Lo! at her death the hedges once more bloomed; and, in spite of snow and frost, fresh roses blossomed in the forest. With these was the pall decked, and on the gentle wings of their fragrance the spirit of the young girl was wafted to the sky.

* * *

A funny story is told of an old lady at Winterich (which we are now passing). The old lady had been the superior of a convent which was suppressed by the French. Much grieved at this, the old lady was seized with fits of melancholy, and when in these fits was in the habit of knocking her head against the table. These knocks being often repeated, and with considerable force, the part thus ill used became hard and horny, until at length a regular ram's horn, with three branches, protruded from the much-knocked head. The old lady cut them down; but they only grew larger and harder, entirely covering one of her eyes. [139]A surgeon being called in, operated on the old dame, who, although now eighty-eight years old, got well through the operation, and lived for two years after, dying in 1836.

The hill called Brauneberg is now passed; the vineyards on it produce a fine wine, called by its name.

At Muhlheim we must leave our river for a time, and explore the charming valley of Veldenz, with its ruined castle placed on the summit of a richly-wooded hill. The walk there is through miles of vineyards edged with fruit-trees, and the valley below the castle is emerald with well-watered grass.

The hills are a mass of forest, and the variously-shaped houses, which are dropped at uncertain intervals along the bubbling stream, form a pleasant picture of rural beauty.

Veldenz was a little principality in itself; formerly it was governed by the Counts of the same name, but afterwards it was given to the church of Verdun, and was then governed by fourteen magistrates, elected by the different villages, and presided over by a prévôt, probably appointed by the Bishop of Verdun.

[Contents]

LEGEND OF VELDENZ.

Irmina wept for her knightly lover, who had departed to fight the Saracens. Her mother bade her dry her tears, for there was no lack of lovers for a pretty girl like her; but Irmina replied with sobs, that the ring which her knight had given her, and which [140]she always wore, united her to him for ever, and seemed to whisper words of love and caress her hand.

Then the mother, fearing for her daughter's health, advised her to throw off the ring, for her lover was surely dead, and it would be wiser to take a live husband than mope for a dead lover.

Persuaded at length, Irmina cast her ring into the well, and seemed to get the better of her melancholy; but one day the ring was drawn up in the well-bucket, and the maid brought it in to her young mistress: then her love likewise returned.

Her mother again persuaded her to cast away the fatal ring, and this time it was buried deep in the earth; but a bean that was buried there likewise, grew rapidly up, and carried the ring to the window of Irmina's chamber.

Much frightened, Irmina yet rejoiced at recovering her ring, and her love for the absent knight grew stronger than ever. Her mother once more pressed her to destroy it, and this time proposed fire as a means of being quit of the ring for ever.

"Do not, dear mother," said the maiden; "'twould be sin before God. In spirit I am wedded to my absent knight, and, alive or dead, none other husband will I have."

Still the mother persisted, and wrested the ring from her daughter's hand; but before she could cast it into the flames the knight stood alive in the room, and soon the ring was used for the purpose of turning the [111]wandering knight and the lady Irmina into a happy bridegroom and bride.

A day's exploration of the Veldenz-thal, and other valleys into which it leads, makes us acquainted with many agreeable walks and charming scenes. The old castle itself is quite a ruin, but well worth exploring, there being still a good deal of its stone-work remaining; vineyards are found within and around its walls.

What enjoyment there is in finding one's self free to climb and saunter amidst delicious scenery! Now we walk briskly along, returning the "*Guten tag*" of the ever-polite peasants, who enunciate this phrase from the bottom of their throats. The *guten* is not heard at all, and the *tag* sounds as if, in the endeavour to swallow the word, the performer choked, and was obliged, when half-strangled, to gasp it out.

At midday we halt, and luxuriate over our hard-boiled eggs and bread and cheese, with green cloth ready spread, and gushing stream sparkling from the rock. Then, as we lie back musing and dreaming, what strange thoughts of the old times come into our heads! Peopled by fancy, the old towers and walls again re-echo to the lutes and voices of long-gone days.

And what a charming friend or mistress we find in Fancy! Most beautiful of aërial beings, she gilds for us the darkest paths, and smiles through every cloud upon her admiring followers.[112]

FANCY.
I climb the hill,
And sit me in the shade;
Sitting I muse,
And, musing, woo the maid
Whose steps earth fill
With flower and loveliness
For those who use
Her kindness not amiss.
She softly sends
To me the gentle gale;
My brow she cools
With scented sweets, that sail
From where she bends
The tree-tops down below,
Mid which in pools
The tiny brooklets flow.
I woo her, she gently kisses me—
Thus goes day, as happy as can be.

46

Great peaks of jagged rock start out of the green hills that surround Burg Veldenz. The stream at its base glitters through the foliage; and the neat, well-kept farm-houses (unusual in this part) that are sprinkled through the valley, make "Thal Veldenz" a perfect Arcadia.

Re-embarking at Muhlheim, and continuing our descent of the river, into which three or four streams now now from the side-valleys, we soon get a sight of the ruined castle above Berncastel, and rounding the island opposite to Cus, the town itself, with its picturesque houses and towers, comes into view.

Muhlheim is celebrated in verse for the sorrows of [143]three sisters, who, as young ladies will do, fell in love, one after another, as each came to years of indiscretion. The eldest, being forbidden to marry by her father, died in three months; the second, being also forbidden, was obliged to be confined in a mad-house; still the unrelenting old father treated his third and youngest daughter in the same harsh manner, objecting to her very natural wish to marry a brave young esquire: having more spirit than her sisters, or being warned by their fate, this youngest ran away with her sweetheart, and was disinherited by the old curmudgeon, who seems to have loved nothing but his gold. We are not told the after-fate of the youngest, or whether love made up for loss of gold.

[144]
[Contents]

CHAPTER XI.

Berncastel by Moonlight.

Berncastel is a delightful, old, tumble-down-looking conglomeration of queer-shaped houses; a mountain-stream hurries through its principal street, if such a heterogeneous jumble of odd gable-ends and door-posts may be called a street: but as it does duty for one, it must receive the appellation.[145]

This street should rather be spoken of in the past tense, for the greater part of it was burnt in 1857; three times the town was on fire in this year, a church and about forty houses being consumed in the last and largest conflagration. As we shall have to revert to these fires again, suffice it to say that the part of the old street nearest the mountain was destroyed.

Berncastel contains some four thousand inhabitants; the tourist passing in a steam-boat would hardly believe so many people were housed in so small a space. This remark will apply to most of the towns and villages on the Moselle, for only a few of the better class of houses are visible from the water in general, the mass of buildings being huddled out of observation as much as possible, and crowded under the base of the impending hills; formerly these Burgs were all walled, which accounts for the crushing.

This town dates from the tenth century, and at the end of the thirteenth it was destroyed by a fire, in which the château of the Bishop was burnt, together with many pictures and other valuable objects, to the estimated worth of 70,000 rix thalers; it is now inhabited by many rich people, to whom a great part of the fine vineyards of the vicinity belong: there are also mines of gold, silver, copper, and lead, which serve to enrich the community.

The vineyards are very extensive, and produce a very good wine; they cover the mountain to a height of some hundreds of feet, and extend for miles down the river. We are shown the estimation in which the [146]Berncasteler wine was formerly held in the following story of

[Contents]
THE BEST DOCTOR.

The lord of the château of Berncastel sat with his Chaplain drinking his wine,—not sipping it, but pouring down huge bumpers, as was the custom then.

Seeing his Chaplain did not drink, the Baron pressed him to do so, assuring him that the fine Muscatel-Berncasteler would be good for his health.

The Chaplain sighing, refused, saying, "It was not meet that he should be drinking while his Bishop lay sick in the town at their feet."

"Sayest thou so!" cried the Baron; "I know a doctor will cure him;" and quaffing down another mighty flagon he set off to the Bishop, carrying a cask of the precious wine upon his own shoulders.

Arrived at the palace, he induced the invalid Bishop to consult the doctor he had brought with him: the invalid tasted, and sipped, then, finding the liquor was good, he took a vast gulp, and soon a fresh life seemed glowing within him.

"That wine restores me," quoth the Bishop. "In truth, Sir Baron, thou saidst well; it is the best doctor."

From that time the Bishop's health mended, and returning again and again to the great phial—for he was in nowise afraid of its size—he soon was quite cured; and ever after he consulted this doctor when feeling unwell, keeping him always within easy reach.

Since this wonderful cure many patients have [147] imitated the example of the venerable Bishop, and a single barrel of Berncasteler-Muscateler is considered sufficient to cure an ordinary patient. More must, however, be taken by those who require it; and in all cases it has been observed, that the patient so loves his good doctor he never is willing to be separated from him for long. "Come and try the Doctor Wine, O ye who suffer under a vicious system of sour beer!"

The little openings in Berncastel, for we cannot call them squares, are rich in subjects for the painter of old houses; they look as if they had walked out of one of Prout's pictures, and set themselves up like stage-scenes for the oddly-costumed people to walk and talk between.

Old Houses in Berncastel.

[148]

A good view is got from the ruined castle over the town; which not in itself very interesting, is yet, on this account, well worth a walk. When there, Cus lies at our feet, with the river rolling between us and it. This Cus (pronounced Koos) was the birthplace of the celebrated Cardinal Cusanus, who, report says, was a fisherman's son: this is, to say the least of it, very uncertain; but doubtless he was born in quite a low station of life, and by his abilities raised himself to be Bishop of Brixen in the Tyrol, and a Cardinal.

He died in 1464; his body rests at Rome, and his heart is deposited in the church of the Hospital which he founded at Cus, for the maintenance of thirty-three persons who were to be not less than fifty years of age, and unmarried; or if married, their wives were to go into a convent.

Of these thirty-three, six are ecclesiastics, six nobles, and twenty-one bourgeois; they all dine at a common table, and wear a like habit of grey; they are presided over by a Rector, who is to be always a priest of irreproachable manners, a mild and good man, and not less than forty years old: all the inmates take a vow of chastity and obedience to the orders of their superiors.

The Inn in Berncastel is a fair sample of the houses of refreshment on the Moselle: the landlord dines with his guests; the dinner is good, but ill-served, and is eaten at one o'clock, being followed by supper at eight. Travellers come and go without the people of the house seeming to care whether they [149] stop long time or short; they are charged according to their nation, English paying more than French, and Germans less than either: however, the charges are not at all high, except for private dinners and out-of-the-way things.

The original pie-dish bason is here found in full force, accompanied by small square boards of napkins; the scantiness, combined with the hardness of which, render them about as useful as a wooden platter would be for the purpose of drying your face,—which, owing to the fortunate construction of the bason, does not, luckily, become very wet.

An agreeable fellow-diner informed us, that on the Moselle two codes of law were in force,—the Prussian on the right bank, and the Code Napoléon on the left: thus, in Berncastel a couple could not be united in marriage without a church ceremony, while in Cus it was optional. Our informant added that the ladies generally insisted on a church marriage, not because they thought the ceremony necessary, but to show off the grand array of their wedding-finery.

48

A tale is told at Cus of a Ghost who haunts the neighbourhood, and sometimes visits the town; he is called

[Contents]

THE BAD MAURUS.

The departed Maurus, who now figures as a pernicious hobgoblin, was formerly a resident of Cus; a drunkard and scoffer at all things holy, this wretch filled up the measure of his iniquities by [150] beating his wife: so ill did he use her, that the neighbours were constantly obliged to come in and save her from his brutality.

The thread of his evil life was summarily cut in this manner: one night as he returned, drunk as usual, to his home, fully intending to beat his wife if waiting up, and equally bent on thrashing her if she had gone to bed, a man in black with a lantern kindly offered to show him the way home: he eagerly accepted the offer, and his guide preceded him; so the two went on, the black-hearted man led by the man in black.

In the morning Maurus was found lying dead at the foot of a rock; they raised the body and brought it to his poor wife, who, forgetting all his ill-usage, sorrowed for the death of her husband.

The widow ordered a suitable funeral, and the body was laid in the churchyard, but on coming back from the funeral, Maurus was seen looking from the garret-window, where he had been observing and sneering at his own funeral: everybody was horrified, and Maurus continued to haunt the upper story of his wife's house until three priests exorcised the hobgoblin, and forced him into the country.

Here the mischievous rascal amused himself by shouting to the ferrymen, "Fetch over! Fetch over!" They, thinking it the voice of a voyager, willingly crossed; then Maurus jeered them, clapping his hands: at last the priests attacked him again, and drove him into the forest. Still, at times the wicked Maurus [151] sneaks into town, and sits on the doorstep of his old house, and his voice is yet heard in the forest, where he wanders for ever.

A charming mountain walk of about four miles leads to Trarbach. Up through the vines we climb, no longer wondering where all the wine comes from; above the vines is a bare crest of heath-covered turf, then a steep descent leads into the valley, at the mouth of which Trarbach is placed: but by going this road, beautiful as it is, more interesting scenery is omitted. The distance by river from Berncastel to Trarbach is about fifteen miles, while by land it is only, as we have said, about four, so great are the bendings of the stream; which, however, we shall follow, being by no means tired of her society. It was at Berncastel that the following verses were written, after admiring the lovely effects there produced by the

MORNING MISTS.

I love the river when the sunshine gay
Kisses the waves, which joyful seem to play,
Dancing like elves so merrily around,
Rippling and gurgling with many a happy sound.
I love the river when the dewdrops fall,
When rocks re-echo to the herdsman's call,
Who, as the eve spreads darkly o'er the plain,
Returning, leads his cattle back again.
I love the river at that moonlight hour
When all bad spirits lose their evil power;
Calmly and holily she rides on high,
The waves soft murmur and the zephyrs sigh.
[152]
But most I love thee, O my gentle River!
When at glad morn the mists around thee quiver;
When round and o'er thee the faint-flowing veil
Now falls, now rises with the swelling gale.
As on her wedding morn the blushing bride,
With fleecy veil and white robe seeks to hide
From eager gazers, who in crowds attend,

49

Her beauty, and the very act doth lend
A greater charm, a new and crowning grace,
To which all other lesser charms give place:
Arrayed in veil and robe of pure white, she
Fit emblem is of virgin modesty.

O thy great beauty! thy enduring grace!
To which all other scenes and streams give place;
Causing all those who thy sweet waters know,
To praise their God, "from whom all blessings flow."

|153|

CHAPTER XII.

The Gräfenburg.

Early rising is absolutely indispensable to the tourist on the Moselle. The steamers constantly start at five or six in the morning, and if walking, the midday heat is too great to be encountered; added to which, he would lose his pleasant rest-time by the sparkling stream.

From Berncastel, then, in the grey of early morning, we wander forth. There are roads on both banks, |154|—small pleasant by-roads, through gardens and vineyards. As we proceed, and begin to think that coffee and new-laid eggs would be no encumbrance, but rather help to balance the system, a faint tinge of crimson appears over the grey hills; little wreaths of mist break away from the mass of watery vapour that clings to the river's banks, and curl upwards to the light, and then with all its glory comes the

BREAK OF DAY.

How beautiful the first faint rays of light,
Gilding the clouds that, banishing the night,
Come like swift messengers, and drive away
From us the darkness, ushering in the day!
The day approaches, brighter and more bright;
The heavens seem bursting with the coming light;
Up flames the sun! and first the lofty hills,
The corn and uplands, with his lustre fills;
The shades retire, the birds melodious sing,
The glad earth turns to meet its gracious King;
Cool blows the wind, the water freshly flows,
All earth rejoices and in sunlight glows.

How strong and full of life we feel as (having break-fasted) we stride along, drinking in with every breath the pure sweet air! *"Guten morgen"* has not yet given place to *"Guten tag,"* and the peasants are ascending to their labour amid the vines; suddenly a strain of martial music fills the air, and all look towards the trees through which now wind a body of soldiers, with their helmets glittering in the light; gaily they march along; the music ceases, and voices take up the strain, |155| which gradually sounds fainter as "the pomp of war" recedes into the distance, until at length the air is left free to the songs of birds.

The birds, the flowers, the trees, the river,—all inoculate our senses with their delights; all claim our praise and thankfulness: but to which shall we award

THE PRIZE OF BEAUTY?

The birds sang, "Unto us the prize
"Of beauty must be given;
"Our songs at morn and evening rise,
"Filling the vault of heaven."
The flowers uplifted their bright heads
From where they had their birth;
"Nay, for our scented beauty sheds

"A charm o'er all the earth."
The trees from ev'ry leafy glade
Their claims with haste expressed;
They urged that they "gave cooling shade,
"'Neath which mankind could rest."
The stream in gentle music said,
"Like birds I sweetly sing;
"Like flowers a charm o'er earth I spread,
"Like trees I coolness fling:
"Thus all their beauties I combine;
"And unto me is given
"A greater glory, for I shine
"With light that flows from heaven."

Where we come to patches of grain-land we find the ploughman busy with his oxen turning up the fresh earth. The oxen are coupled together by short beams of wood, which are fastened to their heads, [156]and must keep the poor animals in a constant state of misery; in other respects the cattle seem well cared for.

Occasionally we meet droves of sheep tended by boys and dogs. The sheep crop a precarious livelihood from the bits of waste land near the river and on the slopes of hills, whose aspect is unfavourable to the culture of the vine.

Arriving at Zeltingen, on the right bank, we taste one of the most delicious wines on the Moselle; it is of a fine rich colour, with a highly-scented flavour, but is withal light and sparkling. In the following incident it will be seen that this wine was properly appreciated by the prebends who owned the Martinshof farm in former days.

[Contents]

THE CASK IN RESERVE.

The fame of the wine made from the grapes that grew in the Martinshof vineyard penetrated even to Trèves, and the Elector Philip was very desirous to drink of a wine so renowned; but the monks, who owned the vineyard, would not take heed of the hints dropped by the Elector on this subject, as they did not love his tyrannical government.

The Elector, therefore, determined, under the pretext of an official inspection, to visit the Cloister.

He accordingly arrived, and the prebends, who had been summoned to meet him, did not fail to make their appearance.[157]

The Abbot perceived that the inspection concerned more his cellar than his cloister. He kept his own counsel, and ordered different sorts of Rhine, Moselle, and Nahe wine to be set before the guests, murmuring the while to himself, "Drink on—drink away, my noble Elector and guests; but the Martinshof wine remains, bright in the cellar: of the mother cask shalt thou never taste."

When the Elector was about to leave he called the Abbot aside, and praised highly the wine he had drunk, and thanked him for his hospitality; he also invited the Abbot to Trèves, but told him he feared he could not give him as good wine as his own Martinshofberger.

The Abbot smiled, thanked him for the compliment, and added, that when the Elector should come to see his *cloister*, not his *cellar*, he would serve to him the *real*Martinshof wine; till then it would be saved for his *true* friends.

The prebendaries and monks were so fond of good wine, that the people suppose their saints must also have a liking for grape-juice; therefore, as soon as the new wine is made each year, a bottle is placed in the hands of the effigy of the Patron Saint, or offered at his shrine: who drinks it eventually, does not appear.

We seem to be quite out of the world on the banks of the Moselle. We wander along amid its ever-varying scenery with that delight which novelty always gives. At every turn new views break upon [158]us; at every step something calls our attention; now it is a flower, then a rock, and again a castle, a group of old houses or trees, or perhaps a little gay boat adorned with boughs of trees, in which children, celebrating a holiday, are singing: so we wander on, and find at midday that, owing to the many detentions caused by these things, and the

51

frequent sketches the beauty of the localities have compelled us to make, we have progressed but little on our road. But what does it matter? we cannot be in a paradise too long; and at every few miles we are sure of finding a little village inn, with a clean room in which we may eat or sleep.

Cloister-Machern is on the left bank of our river, a little further down the stream than Zeltingen. This cloister once contained a lovely nun, named

ERMESINDE.

Antioch had fallen before the Crusaders' arms, and the Cross waved from her towers. The joyful tidings were brought to the banks of the Moselle, and bonfires celebrated the event. The pilgrim who had brought this news from over sea was feasted by Ermesinde's father, and all gathered round him, eagerly catching his words.

He told of the deeds of valour performed by the Christian Knights; and as Ermesinde greedily listened, but feared to question the pilgrim, he mentioned the name of her lover, and highly extolled him, mournfully adding, "Such valour as this Knight showed forth was [159]surpassed by none, but now the grave is closed over his glory."

Hearing, poor Ermesinde fell as though dead, and lay motionless on the stone floor; then the pilgrim saw by the looks of those present that he had incautiously broken her heart. Further interrogating the pilgrim, Ermesinde's father only gained a repetition of the first story told him, and other particulars seemed to confirm it.

The walls of Cloister-Machern received the poor broken reed, who offered to heaven a heart that was dead to the world.

Soon poor Ermesinde found that stone walls do not shut out wickedness, nor sombre dresses cover only morality; for in Cloister-Machern the nuns, one and all, led scandalous lives, and mocked her for not joining with them. She resisted their wiles, and sought refuge in prayer.

One evening a pilgrim arrived at the gate, and asked Ermesinde, who answered the bell, to give him refreshment. As a strain of music, once familiar and dear, the sounds smote on the nun's ear, and with a bewildered look she gazed on the pilgrim's face; the light fell on her pale features, and the pilgrim exclaimed, "Ermesinde!" One long look into each other's eyes and time had vanished, care was forgotten, intervening years had rolled away, and Ermesinde and Rupert were in each other's arms.

Bound by her vows, Ermesinde would not consent to accompany her lover in flight, but she agreed to [160]see him at intervals; and while her sister nuns rioted in the hall she sometimes knelt with Rupert in the chapel, where they prayed for each other's happiness.

When waiting one night for her lover, an old beggar drew near, and prayed for some food. Ermesinde went in to fetch some, but the others refused her request that the old beggar should be relieved, and coming out to him, they drove him away with threats and abuse.

Then the old beggar turned round, and raising his hand to the heavens, cried out: "Woe be unto you, ye false servants of God! chastisement will soon overtake you." So saying, he vanished into the dark cloudy night.

Rupert and Ermesinde were kneeling within the chapel when the storm which was threatening burst forth; fire struck from the clouds on the cloister, destroying the nuns in the hall; the chapel alone was preserved.

Ermesinde now was persuaded that she was released from her vows, and soon she pledged them to Rupert, and as his loved wife she worshipped her God and performed all her duties far better than those who uselessly shut themselves up from the world.

A curious old robbers' nest is still to be seen in the Michaelslei, which is a tall red cliff, a mile or two further on. It consists of a cave, with a strong wall built over its mouth. No path used to lead there, and [161]long ladders were used by the robbers, who, drawing them up after them, were in perfect security.

This castellated cave was once used as a prison, in which an Archbishop was placed; this was the good Bishop Kuno, who was on his road to Trèves, where he was to be installed as Archbishop.

52

The prebends of Trèves wished not to have Kuno for their Archbishop. They, therefore, excited Count Theodorich, who was governor of their town, to send out armed men and capture the Bishop.

Accordingly, when halting at Kylburg, the Bishop, who was travelling in company with the Bishop of Spires, was seized and carried off to the Michaelslei fortress, and there thrown into a dungeon.

Many days the good Bishop languished in his damp cell. At length four ruffians entered and carried him forth to the top of the rock; there binding his limbs, they addressed him as follows: "We have brought you here to see whether you are, indeed, elected of God; as if so, no harm will befall you." Thus jeering, they threw him down into the valley; but the Bishop sustaining no hurt, they twice repeated their deed.

Finding he was not thus to be slain, they ended by killing him with their swords, and cut off his head.

The good Bishop was laid in a tomb, and many miracles were there performed. These coming to the ears of the Count Theodorich, his conscience smote him, and he took the cross and proceeded to the Holy Land. The vessel, unable to uphold his guilty weight, [162] sank down, and the waters now shroud the remains of this wicked Count.

Rounding the promontory on which the Wolf's Cloister is buried in trees, our river's course turns for awhile in the direction of its source, so much does it wind. The Wolf Cloister is only a ruin, of which but little remains.

At a small chapel near here the Pastor of Traben used to perform a service on each Tuesday after Pentecost, and here gathered crowds from all parts to attend at the ceremony. All were covered with flowers, and the young of both sexes pelted each other with bouquets, and dancing and merriment occupied all. But now, says the narrator (Storck), the convent and the sanctuary are no more; their place is filled with vineyards. The present age respects nothing but gold; popular fêtes, sanctuaries, souvenirs of antiquity, and rustic simplicity, are alike swallowed up, and all is sacrificed for money.

A wonderful story is told of a young lady of these parts. One fine day in summer, a very beautiful girl of the family of Meesen was sitting at her open window, engaged in knitting. She was so occupied with her work or her thoughts, that she did not perceive the fearful storm that was rising over the mountains, until suddenly there came a clap of thunder that shook the whole house. Arising in haste, the "fräulein" endeavoured to shut to the window; but before she could accomplish her object a thunderbolt fell, and striking the metal-work which adorned the laces that [163] fastened her bodice, it passed through her garments, softening the metal clasps of her garters, and partially melting her shoe-buckles; then, without having harmed the fair fräulein, it burst its way out by the floor.[1]

Very high hills are surrounding us as we approach Trarbach, a beautifully wooded slope, and rich cliffs announce a site of more than ordinary beauty; but before we take our evening's rest in Trarbach we must, landing at Riesbach, climb to the top of Mount Royal.

This fortress was made by Vauban for Louis XIV. It cost an immense sum of money, and people from all parts were collected and forced to work at its ramparts; but sixteen years after its completion it was dismantled in compliance with treaties, and only a few mounds and walls now mark the site.

Splendid views are seen from it on all sides. The river, starting from our feet, appears gliding in all directions; and the evening shadows are filling the valleys and climbing the hills, while the glory of the departing sun hangs yet upon the corn-fields.

MOUNT ROYAL.

Upon the Royal Mount I stood,
The day was waning to its close;
Soon the great "Giver of all good"
Would send to weary man repose.
[164]
The glorious brilliancy of day
Now soon would leave the world to rest;
And speed on glowing wings away,
To shine on regions further west.

Beneath my feet, the haunts of men
With many sounds of eve were teeming;
The herds returning home again
Drank where the river's tide was gleaming.
Beside me were the wrecks of power
That had been grasped by hand of man;
Around me was that evening hour,
Reminding me how short the span
Of life which kingly pomp and pride,
Though strong on earth, yet vainly tries
To lengthen or to set aside,
When dying on his couch he lies.
Throw down thine iron sceptres then, O kings!
Lift up thy feet from off thy people's necks;
No longer look on fellow-men as things,
Whose toil enriches and whose labour decks
Thy fleeting pomp, thy quickly-passing pride,
Which leaves thee but a worm when life decays;
When no proud robe thy earthly dust shall hide,
And vanished be the pomp of former days.
Like this dead king, whose ruined forts surround,
Lay not up on earth what ye deem glory,
But store that which hereafter may be found
Immortal crowns and thrones to set before ye.

[165]

1This extraordinary incident is related as a simple matter of fact, which is well known in these parts.

[Contents]

CHAPTER XIII.

Trarbach.

Trarbach was an interesting little town, of perhaps fifteen hundred inhabitants. It was one of the most perfect specimens of its class existing, and the fire that burnt it to the ground has robbed many a tourist of subjects for his sketch-book that can scarcely be replaced.

The streets of the town were very narrow and winding, the houses projected over their bases in every variety of irregularity: they were nearly all built of wood frames, filled up with plaster, as those in the villages are; but frequently this plaster was covered with many-coloured tiles, rounded at the edges. The general effect was a sort of green shot with red tints, [166]and being glazed, these tiles reflected blue from the sky, and broken lights and hues of all sorts, giving a very gay and pleasing appearance. The casements were filled with glass that was nearly as green as the tiles, and from the windows hung out lengths of cloth; or bright flowers in their pots filled the openings, when not occupied by the faces of gossips, who carried on quick conversation with others below in the street, or else in the opposite windows, almost within reach of their arms.

A little canal wound about, following the course of the streets. This was covered over with flat stones; but many apertures allowed your feet to slip in, if a careful watch was not kept. The pavements required the same caution, as holes were abundant, and cabbage-stalks plentiful.

Here and there houses more modern, or of greater pretension than others, had large windows and walls built of stone. The church was placed on an eminence, and had many gables, quite in keeping with the little walled town over which it presided. Squeezed into a space too small for its wants, the town overlapped the old walls and formed different suburbs, the chief of which lay on the banks of a brook which here dashes down through the steep valley into the river.

54

Busy and flourishing, Trarbach was quite a gay city compared to the clusters of houses that call themselves Stadts and Dorfs on the banks of our river, and in the valleys surrounding.

High up on a lofty cliff directly over the town are [167]the ruins of the Gräfinburg Castle. In bygone days this castle belonged to the powerful Counts of Sponheim, and was built with funds procured in the following manner from an Archbishop of Trèves, and named after the sharp-witted Countess.

THE BISHOP'S RANSOM.

The Count of Sponheim dying, his beautiful wife, Lauretta, was left with her young son to contend against the malice of the Archbishop Baldwin of Trèves, who claimed her territory for himself, with no right but that of "the strong hand;" Baldwin deeming that a young widow would not be able to support the claims of her son against an Elector and Prince-Bishop.

The Archbishop formally excommunicated her as a first step, on her contumaciously refusing to surrender her rights to a usurper. The beautiful Countess laughed at this proceeding, and being assisted by many good knights, defied all his efforts.

One fine day in May, the Bishop, who was lodging in Trarbach, embarked in a boat for Coblence, and much enjoying the voyage, stood talking and planning with his adherents how best he might surprise the Countess of Sponheim, whose castle of Starkenburg rose from the rocks overhead.

While thus scheming, the Bishop perceived on the bank a number of men, who seemed armed, and awaiting his coming. Hastily, therefore, his lordship gave orders to quicken their pace; but suddenly a great [168]shock threw Baldwin and many of his friends down on their knees. This was caused by the bow of the boat coming quickly against a strong chain, which was placed by the Countess's orders just under the water, reaching from shore to shore. Before the Bishop and friends could recover their footing the Countess's adherents were on them, and the whole party made prisoners and marched up to the Castle of Starkenburg.

The angry Bishop was led into the presence of the beautiful lady. At first the Prelate demanded that he should instantly be freed, and spoke of the rights of the Church, the shameless treachery of the whole proceeding, and the risk his captors ran of damnation.

At all this the lady but smiled, and the Bishop's heart melted within him as he gazed on her beauty.

The days sped away, and the Archbishop Baldwin finding the beautiful Countess was not to be moved by his threats, nor yet won by his love, bethought him at length of his people, who pined for so gentle a shepherd; therefore he sent off to Trèves, asking his flock for a ransom, which the Countess insisted his lordship should pay before he set out, "as some slight compensation," she said, "for the loss of his presence. Moreover," her ladyship added, "that the Archbishop was something indebted for the use of her larder and cellar."

The bill for eating and drinking proved heavy, and the amount for the loss of his pleasing society brought the sum total up to sufficient to pay for the [169]building the strong castle, whose ruins now crumble over the good town of Trarbach: this castle proved an effectual barrier against the Archbishop's encroachments.

At parting, the Prelate absolved the fair Countess of guilt, and took away the excommunication under which she had laboured; so there is probably no truth in the tale that her ladyship haunts the old ruin, and constantly weeps for her crime of incarcerating so holy a man.

This castle of Gräfinburg was a most important fortress, and capable of making a stout resistance, even in the days of cannon; for, in 1734, the Marquis of Belle-Isle was sent by Louis XIV., with a strong army, to ravage the territories of the Elector of Trèves, who escaped by flight to Ehrenbreitstein. The Marquis laid siege to Trarbach, and after a hard struggle, and enduring a fierce bombardment, the garrison capitulated, and marched out with all the honours of war: the castle was then rased to the ground by the Marquis, leaving only the portion engraved at the head of the preceding chapter.

The burning of Trarbach, which happened last autumn, was a splendid but melancholy sight; we chanced to be sleeping at Traben, a town on the opposite side of the river, and from our windows we saw the magnificent spectacle.

About four in the afternoon the fire first began, caused (it was said) by some children playing with [170]matches. As may be easily imagined, from the fact of the very old houses, all built of wood, being crushed into narrow streets and enclosed within walls, the flames spread rapidly; so fast, indeed, they came on, that the poor people flying were forced to throw down the goods they were trying to save and run for their lives. The church, being on an eminence a little out of the town, was thought quite secure, and in it were stored the effects from the neighbouring houses until it was filled from roof-tree to floor.

The night now set in dark as pitch; still the fire crept on, reaching its red forked tongue over the narrow streets, in spite of the water which was freely supplied from the river; at last the church caught, and the flames, bursting from windows and roof, consumed all the goods that were stored, and destroyed the old building itself.

Trarbach in flames.

[171]
The sight was superb; the whole space, enclosed by the hills in which the town lay, surged in great waves of fire: in this huge molten sea great monsters appeared to be moving, whose shapes seemed writhing with pain as those of the devils in hell.

The glare fell on the ruins of Gräfinburg, and the water reflected it back. The houses were all burnt to the ground, excepting only those seen in the view, and a very few others which lay in the outskirt. The inhabitants laboured all night with the engines, but at six in the morning, when we came away, great clouds of dull smoke still ascended from where Trarbach had stood, but which now was only a ruin.

This fire was one of a series. In three succeeding days, Zell, Zeltingen, and Trarbach were more or less burnt; and within a short time Berncastel was thrice visited by the Fire-fiend. Many other smaller fires also took place, and no one could give us the reason; troops were sent out from Trèves, but nothing was ever elicited.

Traben, which was also partially burnt, is a curious enough place, and has as bad pavement as any in Europe: the little inn there was well spoken of by Murray, so now they charge very dear, and give very indifferent food. When we speak of dearness on the Moselle, we do not mean actually dear, for prices are far lower than those on the Rhine; only when in one little inn we get our supper and bed, with bottle of wine, for three shillings, we grumble at paying five for the same in another, where nothing is better.[172]

Not far from Traben is the place where Kloster Springiersbach formerly stood in a solitude; here came crowds of pilgrims, for the place was most holy, and inhabited by many pious monks: of one of these a legend is told, called

[Contents]
THE LILY IN THE CHOIR.

A very pious monk lay dying upon his bed, around him his brethren prayed for his soul; the dying man suffered from much pain, therefore his dissolution would be a blessing for him. The monk had been too weak to attend at his prayers in the chapel for many days past, and lo! over the place where he had been accustomed to pray, a white lily put forth its leaves. The holy man died, and the lily then burst into flower: so passed the guileless soul of the man from earth into heaven, and the pure blooming lily long marked the place where he knelt in the chapel,—an image of him whose departure from earth we now have narrated.

[173]
[Contents]

CHAPTER XIV.

Marienburg.

Still surrounded by very high hills, the course of our river winds onwards past Starkenburg, from which the Countess pounced down on the crafty Archbishop. The pathway to Enkirch extends, under fruit-trees, a little way inland, to where the ferry-boat crosses the river.

Passing from Bertrich to Traben one day, we heard, on arriving near Enkirch, sounds of music and [lo]llowing of cattle. People in shoals, too, were crossing the river, filling the boats of all sizes. We found it was Fair-day in Enkirch, so, joining a party of brightly-dressed girls, we went over to see all "the fun of the *Fair*."

At these Kermes, or Fairs, the amusements are much like those on similar festivals in England. Goods of all sorts are exposed in little old booths, round which the gossiping purchasers stand. Ribbons and gingerbread, shawls, pottery, and cheap dresses, are the principal objects of purchase; also spikes for the back of the hair of unmarried girls, and little embroidered pieces of velvet or cloth.

The amusements consist chiefly in dancing and drinking; there are not many shows, but "the round-about" plays its full part, and even women and men ride, as well as the children.

The dancing is carried on with the greatest possible spirit; in fact, it seems a matter of duty. The "Schottische," or something very much like it, seems to be the favourite dance; but waltzing in the old style has many adherents.

The girls are smartly dressed, and very lively and pleasant; they and their lovers drink freely of the light wine of the country, and grow a little more lively as the day turns into night.

Strangers at these places are considered as part of the show, and stared at amazingly; but when addressed, the peasants are perfectly civil, and seem glad to talk: they are, for the most part, well informed,—[175] far more so than farm-labourers in England usually are.

When the Kermes is over, the holiday-makers in groups embark in their boats, or walk merrily home, often singing in parts as they go. Some of the men take rather more wine than is good for them, but a quarrel very seldom occurs.

Enkirch.

Enkirch is a small town of 2000 inhabitants, containing nothing remarkable. A great deal of wine is made near there, and its situation is very agreeable; surrounded as it is by hills, the summer showers often break over it, cooling the air, and freshening the sail.[176]

From Enkirch a very pleasant path leads us to Entersburg, famous for the legend of [Continens]

THE VALLEY OF HUSBANDS.

On the heights over the little hamlet of Burg are still to be seen some remnants of an old castle. Here a Robber-Knight once had his residence. This Knight made it his profession to capture all travellers, and carry them off to his dungeon, from which they were only released on procuring a very large ransom.

For a long time this trade was most prosperously carried on, but at length (success perhaps begetting envy, as usual,) a certain nobleman vowed vengeance on the depredator, and swore to destroy him and his castle. For this purpose he set out with a large force, and surrounded the Robber-Knight's tower.

The robbers fought furiously, yet were forced to retreat into their fort by the superior force of the nobleman.

The chief then being short of provisions, consulted his wife (as all prudent men should), and she concocted a plan. The lady then mounted the tower, and addressing the nobleman, said that the stronghold should be given up if he would allow her to carry out a bundle of whatever she wished. To this modest request the besieger readily gave his assent, and the lady came forth with a heavy bundle placed in a basket, which she carried with difficulty.

The besiegers allowed her to pass, and rushed [177]into the fort, slaying the robbers who there were collected.

The lady and bundle were all that escaped; and so this courageous and sharp-witted woman saved the life of her husband.

The valley is still called the Manne-thal, or Valley of Husbands.

Below Burg, on the left bank, is Reil, most charmingly snuggled in trees; a road from it leads up to the forest, through which passes a good road to Alf. This road keeps along the crest of the hill, past the neck of the Marienburg promontory, then descends into Alf.

The views from this road are superb. Through the openings of oak-trees are seen distant landscapes, that, sleeping in sunshine, seem gems to adorn the green girdle which Nature binds round the earth.

The fairy Moselle seems tranquilly sleeping through noontide, while in the heavens the fleecy white clouds are protecting our gentle river from harm; and their brightness reflected in her, seems a sweet dream sent from above, which gladdens the heart of the sleeper.

There is a dip in the long neck of land that leads towards Zell, which enables us to see a distant reach of our river; thus, standing quite still, three different windings are seen, and by taking a very few paces, a fourth (beyond Alf) comes in view.[178]

Comparisons are more or less odious, as every one knows, and has written when young; but, considering the raptures in which people annually indulge on the Rhine, it is, to say the least of it, wonderful that scarcely any visit our lovely river, which certainly will not suffer by being compared with the grander and manlier stream.

The Convent of Marienburg dates from the twelfth century. Owing to its situation, it was always sought by conflicting parties as a strong post in war-time, which so interfered with its usefulness as a place of repose for the weary in mind, that Pope Leo X. had it abolished, and the twelve canonesses received each a pension of twenty-five florins of gold, a half tun of wine, and three sacks of corn; so with these goods of the world they contented themselves for the loss of their convent.

At this present time the ruins of the convent and church are still standing, and within them an inn and a bright little garden, where refreshments are served by the landlady and her two daughters: the father is one of the Foresters, and his house is adorned with arms of all sorts. In the garden is a large room, surrounded with spoils of the chase, and stuffed animals of all sorts and sizes. The young ladies play the guitar and sing national songs, so a day may be pleasantly spent there in the old German style.

There is a little chapel still fitted up; as they open the door the interior is gloomily seen, but a window [179]throws a strong light on a misshapen image of some cadaverous saint. The effect is quite startling, especially if you have been listening to the tales of the hermits and ghosts who delighted to live and to wander here. Here is one of the stories, called

THE PALE NUN.

Over-persuaded by the Abbess and sisters, Marie had entered the convent, forsaking her lover, the Knight Carl of Zant, and all her worldly possessions.

The vows were taken and the days wore on, the kind attentions and former solicitude of the nuns vanished, and poor Marie found her life one long monotony; then she remembered her lover, and the wings of the poor prisoned bird were hurt by the wires of the cage.

At length she bethought her that her possessions, not herself, were the objects desired by the Abbess; so she fell at the feet of this lady, and offered to give all that she had to the convent, if only she might depart. The haughty Superior severely replied, that her goods had all passed to the cloister, and inflicted a penance for the carnal desires that she said were wickedly filling the heart of the nun.

From this time forth Marie rapidly drooped like a poor blighted flower, whose beauty and gladness departed, remains on its stem with bowed head and but a semblance of life.

One morning a fisherman found her dead body at [180]rest within the Moselle. The Knight Carl being informed of her fate set off for the Holy Land, and there died fighting the battles of faith.

The Pale Nun may often be seen, with her wan face lit up by the moon, as she glides noiselessly through forest and ruin.

The ruins are placed on the summit of the neck of land, and Murray's "Guide-book" compares the view at this place to one on the Wye, and with justice; indeed, those who are acquainted with the beautiful Wye will find the Moselle has many points of resemblance to her young sister in England, but she is in every respect more lovely and graceful.

This promontory is about three miles in length, and scarcely five hundred yards across in the narrowest place. It is a spur of the Eifel mountains, or hills, as they are called, according to the fancy of the speaker. The promontory is two or three hundred feet over the bed of the river, and near the ruined cloister the slope is almost precipitous, just affording spaces for vines, which flourish extremely on the south side. The forest extends over the base of the promontory, and then gives place to the corn-fields and meadows.

The Eifel is a volcanic range, which is thrown up in peaks and great rugged masses. Formerly, these were volcanoes or craters, but now they are merely objects of interest in the landscape, shining above the level of the forest, which climbs round their bases. This level varies in height, but is always some hundreds [181] of feet above the river; and from the table-land break little valleys, completely embosomed in trees, and glittering with brooks. In the next chapter we shall visit one of these valleys.

On the upper or south side of Marienburg, and immediately opposite, is Punderich, famous for nothing except the following legend:—

[Contents]

THE GOLD CROWN.

A little way out of the village of Punderich stands a small chapel, within which, on a stone altar, is a figure of the mother of God. A crown of silver shines on her head, and a white veil flows over her shoulders.

A long while ago the Virgin was crowned with a crown of pure gold; but a wicked knight, named Klodwig, who owned many forts on the banks of the river, passed by. When he was near to the chapel a great storm arose, and the fierce thunder crashed round him. Seeing the chapel he sought refuge there, and guided his horse up to the altar. Thankless for shelter, on perceiving the crown he snatched it down from the image's head, and placed it upon that of his courser.

No sooner was the sacrilege committed than off started the courser, and fled frantically over the fields; the guilty knight, seeing the river before him, endeavoured to throw himself down from his horse, but before he could accomplish his purpose the river [182] received them, and down sank the gold crown, the knight, and his charger.

At the end of the Marienburg promontory, round which we are now passing, is the village of Kaimt, and on the opposite shore stands the bright town of Zell.

Zell is a flourishing place, extending along the bank of the river; its general aspect is cheerful and new, but here and there an old house with little quaint pinnacles reminds us of the age of the place. These little old houses seem squeezed into corners by the pretentious new-comers, whose elbows push into the ribs of the poor old fellows, until their timbers or ribs are bulged out by the pressure.

There is a round tower above, and lines of poplars reach out of the town; the mountain overhead is full of ravines, and bushes of stunted growth here and there appear on the surface. A little higher up stream, where the river turns round, resuming her course to the north, the hills are most beautiful; for, covered with trees, the shadows as the day lengthens creep on, and break into masses the huge cliffs and sons of the forest.

Zell is renowned for the bravery of its inhabitants, which at one time had passed into a proverb.

The village of Kaimt, from whose gardens the vine-wreaths sweep down just over our heads as we pass, was always unlucky; as the weaker in war go [183] to the wall, so, being close to the strong fort of Zell and the fortified cloister of Marienburg, Kaimt was generally burnt by one or other of the contending parties, and always plundered by both.

Merl.

59

Soon we reach Merl, where the Knight Carl of Zant lived, who loved the Pale Nun of Marienburg. Many other distinguished families lived in this town, which is very old, and full of quaint houses; its [184]situation is very delightful: sheltered from cold by the vine-covered mountain behind, it looks out on the bend of the river, with Marienburg opposite and Alf in the distance.

Before arriving at Alf is Bullay. This charming town is celebrated for its fêtes and its gaiety; on one of its fêtes, a noble and numerous company being collected, the host of the party, a relation of the Knight Carl of Zant, filled a huge bumper and asked one of his guests, named Frederick of Hattstein, if he could drink it down at a draught, as he thought he seemed afraid of his wine.

Frederick being a very strong man (not liking to be mocked), seized a full cask that stood in the room and lifted it up; then exclaiming, "I take this draught in honour of the Elector of Trèves, my good master;" he finished the ohme.

Excited by this, and not wishing to be outdone by a stranger, the host and his brother each seized a like cask, and emptied them in honour of the Emperor and the Abbess of Marienburg: these three are still known as the three topers of Bullay.

Without answering for the truth of this story, we believe it is an undoubted fact, that in the "old times" German nobles daily drank a portion of wine equal to about sixteen of our bottles.

We now arrive at Alf.[185]

[Contents]

CHAPTER XV.

Bertrich.

Deep down, within the caverns of the earth,
Reigns Rubezahl, the Gnome;
Here reigned he, long before man had his birth,
Beneath the rocky dome.
Fires glowed around him, and the great hall shone
With fitful glare that from their flames was thrown.
[186]
Diminutive and swart his subject slaves
Grim-visaged stood around,
Collected in all haste from central caves,
Where, delving underground,
Ever these baneful sprites are doomed to toil,
And win from rocky beds their iron spoil.
Met thus within the murky council cave,
The Gnomes and their great King
Agree to stay the course of the pure wave Which now is hastening
From her far mountain source with joyous tide,
To meet her husband Rhine, a fairy bride.
The scheme agreed upon was, by the fire
Enchainèd underground,
To raise within the earth commotion dire;
And thus with rocks surround
The pure stream, which hitherward was flowing
With beauty crowned and with heaven's light glowing.
So with his flame-sceptre King Rubezahl
Causes the earth to shake;
Back flow the streams, the neighb'ring mountains all
With fear and terror quake;
The lurid fires burst forth with horrid glare,
Defacing earth, defiling the glad air.
Thus were the Eifel mountains upwards thrown
From out the deep abyss;

Thus sought the Evil King to reign alone,
Driving from earth that Bliss
Which rapidly was gliding here to dwell
In the sweet person of the bright Moselle.

Joyously onward, from the Vosges hills speeding,
Dances the fairy stream;
Attendant rivulets her course are feeding,
Whose shining torrents gleam[187]
Forth from the valleys, where they timid hide,
To join their life with hers and swell her tide.

Thus flowed she on, until her course was stayed
By the uplifted hills;—
Grim smiled the Fire-king at the fairy maid
And her attendant rills.
The Gnomes peeped forth from many a cavern hole,
And forged fresh fetters to enchain the soul.
Oh, short-lived triumph! never yet was sin
Allowed to conquer long;
Never was bounteous love thus hemmed in
By evil spirits strong,
But it would win its way through hearts or stone,
Causing their power to yield before her own.
So wins her way around, with graceful bend,
The fairy stream Moselle;
And the Gnome King, and all his will attend,
Are forced their wrath to quell;
While she and her enleaguèd fairies throw
Over these Eifel hills, thus raised, a glow
Of more than earthly beauty, which exceeds
All else around her course;
Each Fairy gives her gift—the streamlet leads,
Above the hidden force
Of demons toiling in eternal night,
Its silv'ry thread, for ever glad and bright.
The Wood-Nymphs give their shadiest coverts green,
Spread out fresh turf and flowers,
And clothe the banks which the brooks glide between
With everlasting bowers.
Thus were the rocks thrown upward by the Gnome
Made pleasant spots for future man to roam.
[188]
In the most exquisite of these sweet vales
Gushes a healing fount,
A bounteous spring, whose water never fails
To flow from forth the mount.
Love so has banished Hate, and Beauty shines
Above the darksome toil of demon mines.

From Alf to Bad Bertrich an excellent road runs winding through a succession of green valleys, shut closely in by the mountains, which are covered with foliage. The Alf-bach, or brook, runs by the side of the road; its waters turn the wheels employed in the iron-works, which are embosomed in trees near the entrance of these secluded valleys. So, after all, we find the fire-fiend is not extinguished, but by the assistance of his friend Man is, as of old, still defacing nature and enslaving a beautiful stream.

Six English miles of beauty bring us to Bad Bertrich itself. In all probability, the tourist in Germany will here exclaim, "I never heard of Bad Bertrich." Even so, we reply; and that constitutes one of its greatest charms. While the English, and Russians, and French are all swarming to Baden, to Ems, Schwalbach, Wildbad, and the legion of baths with which all Germany teems, there is left neglected one of the most beautiful places in Europe. There is plenty of shade, and plenty of sun, and plenty of air, and yet "the Bad" is quite sheltered.

The village is very small and clean. There are several small inns, and one good hotel, called Werling's. [189]This hotel is kept by an unmarried woman, who is one of the oddest, best-hearted old bodies possible. She, however, is not the leading person in the establishment, as everything is left to the waiter, a remarkable character.

This waiter is an exceedingly jolly old fellow, who, as the day advances, becomes more and more deeply in liquor; his eyes close up gradually, and his senses seem to be wandering. Now these symptoms are not unusual to men in his state; but it is most unusual for a man when so overcome to be able to wait on some twenty or thirty guests, to bring what is wanted for each, and to (without any notes) keep account in his head of what wine and food each has partaken. Yet all this he does, and does it right well.

In the winter this hotel is shut up, and our old friend the waiter goes hunting with two apoplectic dogs, that snore on chairs all the summer.

While we were there, his waiting, and drinking, and hunting were nearly all brought to a sudden termination; for one night, while sitting at supper, a tremendous smell of sulphur began to pervade the apartment, and following our noses, we found that it came from a small room to which the old waiter retired between courses to indulge in a sip. By this time the smell was so strong, and on opening the door the air became so dense, that it was all we could do to drag the old fellow out. It then appeared that some visitors had given him a parcel of fire-works to put safely [190]aside, and he had *for safety* placed them among matches and candle-ends, and somehow the whole had exploded.

Adjoining the inn is the bath-house, and around it a garden and promenade. Close by is a fountain, where the public drink the waters for nothing. The baths cost one shilling each, and are most delicious. The water flows through all the time you are in, and bubbles and seethes round your body: the after-effect is to freshen and strengthen the frame, while the nerves are all soothed.

The Herr Director is an old officer of engineers or artillery, and speaks excellent English. He is a man of great taste, and has laid out (at the expense of the Government) the walks and extensive grounds of the place.

All over the woods and the valleys these walks wind through the shade; and at all the best points of view are seats of wood or stone, covered with bark. Often, too, summer-houses, with roofs that will keep the showers from wetting the visitors, are met on the hills.

Bad Bertrich was well known to the Romans, who, in the fourth century, erected a bath-house and other fine buildings. Remnants of these are often turned up, and some are preserved.

In the fifteenth century these baths again became noted, but fell again into disuse; but in 1769 the last Elector of Trèves had the springs properly managed, and built the Kurhaus, which now stands.[191]

The bathing establishment, hotel and village, are clustered together at one end of a circular valley. Precipitous cliffs shut in this beautiful valley, round which a brooklet runs singing. The cliffs are covered with forests of oak, beech, and other fine trees. The little paths that wind round them are bordered with mountain-ash, through whose red clusters of berries the green carpet which lies in the valley, with the water splashing around it, is seen.

Two eminences in the green valley are surmounted by the two churches: one is Protestant, and the other (the old one) is for Roman Catholic worship.

A pleasant little society of Germans collect at this place, and music enlivens the air; but the season is considered quite over in September, and the music then goes away.

Water to drink and water to bathe in, and plenty of fresh air and exercise, will render a stay at Bad Bertrich most pleasant; added to which there are plenty of excursions to make, plenty of pleasant walks, and objects to sketch; and wild flowers and rocks to examine; or shooting for those so inclined.

One of the shortest and most beautiful walks about Bertrich is to the Käsegrotte, or cheese grotto: this is a cave supported by basaltic pillars which look as if made of cheeses placed one on the top of the other. By the side of the cave tumbles a rill of water, which flows from a most beautiful little pool above; [192] over the ravine is a rustic bridge, exceedingly well-constructed: the banks are covered with trees.

Käsegrotte.

LINES ON THE KÄSEGROTTE.

Pure and beautiful the streamlet flows,
Fresh from the earth it springs;
Like heavenly light that o'er earth glows,
And fans the angels' wings.
Within the grot a Spirit dwells,
Lovely, and pure, and sweet;
Hard by the streamlet gently wells,
Cooling the fair retreat.

[193]

So, hidden in the heart of man,
Is love for nature pure;
So, ever since the world began,
Has welled God's mercy sure.

Close to this grotto is a seat commanding an exquisite view of the Alf-bach; its course is blocked with masses of stone washed down by its torrent: these stones form the brook into a succession of little pools, in which the setting sun reflects his brightness. Paths along the brook lead through groves in which seats, beautifully placed, are dedicated to different German poets.

Another little spring, called the Peter's Brunnen, on the side of the hill opposite the village, is famous for the extreme clearness and coldness of its waters; the water is collected into a cistern, and sitting in the shade under the rock which holds these cold waters, the air is cool even on the hottest day. A lion's head allows the imprisoned spring to send forth its waters, which trickle and splash into a bason underneath.

LINES ON THE PETER'S BRUNNEN.

Trickling gently, lightly falling,
The Water-Nymph to us is calling
From her hidden cool retreat,
Where the hill-drops fresh do meet;
And to us she seems to say,
"My commands on you I lay,
"That, while thus you near me stay,
"You shall drive all care away,
"And with my waters' murmur sweet
"Refresh your minds at my retreat."

[194]

The meadow that fills the valley of Bertrich is intersected with walks, and gardens are being formed at the end farthest from the village. Above these new gardens the Alf falls in a cascade over the rocks; a part of the water is conducted into fish-ponds, that are to be well stocked.

The Falkenlei is well worth visiting; it is a bare mass of rock, that rears its head over the tree-tops on the summit of a mountain: it is 160 feet high and 600 feet long; it is formed of basalt, and is inhabited by foxes and falcons. It is supposed to be an extinct volcano.

One of the best rambles is down the valley nearly to the village of Alf, and then up the hills to Burg Arras; afterwards, explore the Uesbach valley. But in all directions the walks are nearly equally beautiful, and as only a visit can convey a proper idea of Bad Bertrich, we will not endeavour to bring into mere words such beautiful scenery: go and explore!

The first Knight of Arras was a brave man, who, at the time of the Hunnish invasion, was a poor collier; he had twelve sons equally brave, and they all fought so stoutly and well, that after the defeat of the Huns the Pfalz-graf selected this collier as the bravest and best warrior there, and causing him then to kneel down conferred on him the order of knighthood and gave him this castle.

The Alf-bach, of which we here give a peep, falls into the Moselle at the village of Alf, which is [125]a cheerful old town; as usual, beautifully placed between the river and brook: it contains very good little inns, and is a good point to rest at.

Alf-bach.

EVENING SHADOWS.
The sun retires—the shades draw near—
Their lengthened forms now close appear;
With noiseless step they onwards speed,
Like Time, whose passage swift we heed
As little as the close of day,
Which vanishing from us away
Leads surely to eternity.
[126]
Oh, let the waning daylight teach
This lesson; whilst yet Time can reach,
Ere from our eyes is passed for ever
That day which life from death doth sever,—
"From earthly shadows let us fly,
"Let upwards soar our thoughts on high,
"To where Love reigns eternally."

The Old Church.

[127]
[Contents]

CHAPTER XVI.

Beilstein.

The steamers that ply on the Moselle are few in number, but very well appointed. Sometimes in summer there is not enough water to enable them to [128]travel, and often a good bump is experienced from some hidden rock. On one occasion we knocked quite a good-sized hole in the bottom, and tore off a large piece of one paddle-wheel; but there was not the slightest danger, as the water was not deep enough for us to sink into it, so we pumped away for some time, and patched up the hole. Shortly after we met the down-steamer, which had likewise started a leak, and we were all much amused at the solemnity with which our captain handed over to his friend a pump, which he knew would not work, as he had tried it in vain in our boat. It was received with gratitude.

There was a waiter on board this boat, whose sole object in life seemed to be to cheat the passengers; his powers of *addition* were very great, and only surpassed by his effrontery. There is a printed tariff for everything, so his attempts were generally unsuccessful; but, like a gallant fellow, he returned again and again to the charge, nothing abashed; we frequently met this individual, and although he must, after the first two or three attempts, have found out that we were not to be done by him, yet up to our last settlement he tried to overcharge; poor fellow, it was, we suppose, an innocent mania, like some people have for pocketing lace. The living is good, and the boats not at all crowded, which is better for the passengers than the Company; and the officers are very polite.

A straight reach of the river brings us to Neef, which is completely embosomed in trees, and the hills at its back are covered with vines. On the opposite [129]bank the bare rock abruptly approaches the water; from it a road has been blasted.

Neef.

The Government are yearly improving the navigation of our river, by blowing up rocks and damming the stream.

There is a legend connected with Neef, nearly similar to that of St. Brelade's Church in Jersey, which we have already laid before our readers in *Channel Islands*. The following is the Moselle version:—

[Contents]

THE ANGEL WORKMEN.

On the hills above Neef is a graveyard, still used for its original purpose. In this formerly stood a chapel, which was built here for the following reasons:—[200]

In olden times the chapel of Neef fell into a ruinous state, and collections were made all about the Moselle country to enable the village to rebuild their chapel. The holy communities in the neighbourhood gave liberally, and soon sufficient being collected, the work was begun.

To the surprise of the builders, every morning they found their yesterday's labour undone, and the stones and other materials carried up to where the graveyard now is.

The Pastor ordered night-watches to guard the new works, and punish the guilty offenders.

The night closed around them, and the hours wore on without anything happening to alarm the watchmen, when suddenly one exclaimed that the stars were moving towards them. The eyes of all then beheld luminous flakes, which, coming nearer and nearer, grew into angels, with bright shining wings, and love on their brows.

The angels approached and gathered the stones, then bore them to the hill-top, after which they receded again into heaven.

The materials thus consecrated were used for the purpose so clearly pointed out, and the chapel was raised on the top of the hill, instead of being hid in the valley beneath.

A sharp turn to the left brings us to Bremm, an old rotten town, with a good church. The people of Bremm seem more squalid than those of any other [201] town on the Moselle; whether they merely wish to be in keeping with their houses or not, we did not ascertain.

Opposite Bremm is a fair promontory, on whose sloping green turf the ruins of Kloster Stuben are seen. The hills on the left-hand bank bend round in the form of a horse-shoe, and the river flows at their base. The hills are very superb, of considerable height; and their grand sombre mass contrasts with the green fields around Kloster Stuben.

This horse-shoe form constantly occurs on the Moselle; and not only is the bend of the stream in the form of a horse-shoe, but the enclosed space is usually shaped precisely as it would be had it been formed of soft lava, and stamped by the gigantic foot of a horse. Perhaps the Wild Huntsman rode here while the volcanoes were still in full force.

The first Abbess of Kloster Stuben was Gisela the Fair; her father, a knight, built the cloister, and endowed it as a resting-place for his poor daughter Gisela, who thus lost her lover:—

[Contents]

GISELA.

The fair Gisela sat in her bower, waiting impatiently for her knightly bridegroom.

The sun watched with her all day, but at last, growing weary, sank westwards.

Still Gisela watched—for love never wearies—and at length she had her reward; for, rounding the cliffs, a noble bark came gallantly on, and nearer and nearer [202] it glided until she could see her loved knight, who stood looking eagerly up.

On seeing Gisela he shouted, and all his friends waved their hands. His ardour could not be restrained to the vessel's slow motion, and landwards he sprang to embrace his fair bride; but the leap was too great, and the good knight sank down, overpowered by the weight of his armour, and never rose more.

Gisela wept not, but her bosom became cold as the waters that closed over the head of her lover, and she passed from the world into the cloister of Stuben.

Another legend of Kloster Stuben we may call

[Contents]

A LIBEL ON NIGHTINGALES.

The monks of Himmerode led dissolute lives, and Saint Bernard was sent to reprove them, and endeavour to bring them back to a sense of their duty.

In vain the Saint lectured—the monks were wicked as ever, and the Saint in despair sought his chamber; there, opening his window, he sat down to plan fresh arguments with which he might touch the wicked hearts of the monks.

The music of the sweet nightingales swelled up to his ears, and steeped his senses in bliss; but the Saint perceived, to his horror, that wicked desires then arose in his breast: so, closing the window, he hastened away. The thought then occurred to the Saint that, if the songs of the nightingales thus affected so holy [203]a man as himself they must do infinite harm to the monks; he therefore (having the power) banished the birds, and shortly the monks were reformed.

The Abbess of Stuben, who gently ruled over a religious body of nuns, hearing the nightingales had been driven out, and were wandering in search of a home, invited them to settle in the meadows and groves that surrounded her cloister.

The birds gladly arrived, and their songs, which had harmed the wicked monks' hearts, cheered and exalted the thoughts of the pure-hearted nuns.

Nuns and nightingales are now alike departed, as well as the droning old monks, whose notes we could better have spared.

Kloster Stuben.

[204]
There is a fine view from the cliffs behind the cloister, and the walk hence to Beilstein is very agreeable, as the banks are all richly wooded, and of a great height.

The river winds on past many a hamlet and burg; the forests and vines succeed to each other; islands are passed, and the scene constantly changes; spires rise among trees, old houses peep forth, cattle wade in the stream, and our little skiff glides along until Beilstein Castle appears, so beautifully placed, and so charmingly surrounded by forest, that we at once stay the course of our boat, and pull out our sketch-books. The townlet is nestled in walls, which are adorned with several turrets, and over it stands up the sharp-pointed spire of a church: the castle presides above all.

A great load of bark is slowly drifting down our river's sparkling tide, and the boats are crossing and recrossing, filled with busy husbandmen.

Where our boat now stands, once a gentle peasant girl found her death and grave together, and with the latter peace, we trust.

[Contents]
THE SHIPMASTER'S DAUGHTER OF BEILSTEIN.

Kuno of Beilstein was struck with the beauty of a shipmaster's daughter. She heard and responded to his love, believing the words that he spoke.

The innocent dove cannot stand any chance with the hawk; so the poor girl after a time found out, to her cost, when Kuno forsook her.[205]

Madness seized on the brain of the wretched girl, and for a long time her senses were wandering; but one morning in spring her memory returned, and she begged her father to take her where she might gaze on the castle of her false betrayer, for she loved him still.

Her father, who truly loved her, placed the poor girl in a boat, and rowed up the river to where a good view of the castle was gained. She gazed with tears on the spot, and prayed for the welfare of Kuno.

While gazing, a sound of horns and of dogs swept down the valley, and as the shouting grew nearer Count Kuno was seen, with his young haughty bride riding near him. Kuno, at seeing the girl in the boat, started, and uttered her name. The young bride grew jealous, and questioned the Count as to what he knew of the girl. He replied, she was nothing to him; and, to pacify her, launched an arrow at his former love.

The shot took effect, and the father, rushing to save her, overbalanced the boat, and both father and daughter sank down for ever.

66

Beilstein is not over-clean, although a stream runs through it; but then it is the essence of picturesqueness, which more than makes up. It seems to have been in former days a place of some importance, but with the decay of the castle the town itself has decayed, and the walls crumble down, and the houses are empty.

Many Jews live here, and it is said the dark-eyed [206] Jewesses are very beautiful, and extremely inquisitive about strangers, asking them many questions.

A series of valleys—all wooded, and watered, and pleasant—lie at the back of Beilstein. Unfortunately the inns are very poor, so it is not a good place to stop at; but if not very fastidious, the accommodation will suffice for two or three nights; and the white wine is good.

There still remain considerable portions of wall and fragments of towers of the castle of Beilstein. Its situation is very happily chosen for both beauty and strength. On the side over the town an ascent is impossible. A narrow ridge connects the castle with the neighbouring mountains; along this ridge is a path, which conducts us through fruit-trees and vineyards to an old burial-ground, filled with tombstones with Hebrew inscriptions. Here the Jews are buried apart.

On the opposite side of our river is Poltersdorf, or the village of blustering fellows; so called, because its inhabitants were always quarrelling with those of the neighbouring hamlets.

The scenery from Beilstein to Cochem is not to be surpassed on our river. There are mountains, beautiful churches and villages, trees, rocks, and water, with happy faces smiling from under their picturesque head-dresses.

Arriving at Cochem, Herr Paoli, who talks French, and his wife, who talks English, will attend to your comforts at the Hôtel de l'Union. [207]

[Contents]

CHAPTER XVII.

Cochem by Moonlight

The moon shines bright o'er vale and hill,
O'er castle wall and donjon keep;
Her beams they dance on every rill,
On every turret seem to sleep.

[208]

Such was the hour and such the night on which the mad Pfalz-graf, Henry of Cochem, slew his wife. Thus runs the tale in the overture:—

[Contents]

LEGEND OF COCHEM.

The Pfalz-graf Henry, called "the Mad," had a bitter quarrel with the Archbishop of Cologne, and had been worsted in combat with the Archbishop's troops; retiring, he shut himself up in his castle of Cochem.

As the evening drew on, the Pfalz-graf became more and more excited, and strode to and fro in his chamber. The light of the full moon still further added to his fury, and he raged like a lion confined in his den, constantly calling on the Archbishop by name, and vowing vengeance against him.

His gentle wife approaching him sought to soothe him with her caresses, and addressed him with words of endearment. For a few moments he seemed to be calmer; but then starting up, he seized a great axe and struck his wife to the earth.

At seeing this monstrous deed, the attendants sprang forward; alas! too late, for the gentle lady was dead.

The madman was seized and taken to the Archbishop of Trèves, who had him confined in a cell, where he soon after died.

The town of Cochem is hid by the trees on our left as we look at the castle: it contains about 2500 inhabitants, [209] and is a very clean, flourishing town. It contains very fair shops, and the hotel is good. It is very picturesque; its streets are steep and narrow, and the old walls and gate-towers add to its general appearance of age. On market-days it is crowded with people from all the adjoining villages, who sell their produce to dealers who supply the market of Coblence. A little steamer bustles and puffs down the stream into Coblence every day, and gets back again in the evening.

Cochem is a good resting-place, as in its neighbourhood are found many interesting places, such as Beilstein, Marienbourg, Clotten, Treis, Elz, &c.; and immediately around it the country walks are very numerous, varied in character, and beautiful.

Sitting in the balcony of the inn, too, is very pleasant; the steamers, with their passing life, arrive and depart just opposite; the great fleets of barges are pulled past by dozens of horses, at which the drivers scream and crack their whips till the whole valley resounds; fishermen ply their trade, and at night-time light fires on the banks, that thus they may be able to see their prey in the water.

Opposite is a small village, and behind this village are vineyards belonging to Cochem; so the constant communication necessarily kept up makes the river appear very lively. Boats also are generally being built or repaired, and the girls are washing linen or carrying water up from the stream.

Between Cochem and Beilstein there is, at a turn [210]of the river, a beautiful cemetery, and a church with twin-spires. The cliffs and river sweep round the angle and shut in this retired nook, which, thus separated from the world, appears a fit resting-place for those whose waking will be in a world more glorious than this. There are on our river many cemeteries and graveyards, most beautifully placed; and the graves, with their simple crosses, seem the realisation of peace.

Nearer to Cochem is a very perfect echo; it repeats twice with great clearness, and is so long before answering that there is time to say quite a sentence. Thus it invited us to "come again to-morrow;" and for many a morrow we visited and revisited the scenery here, the endless foot-paths over rocks and through vines, or forests, or fields, ever giving us new views and fresh combinations of beauty, and we found days pass into weeks with the greatest rapidity.

Following the brook at the end of the town, we arrive at the foot of the hill on which the strong castle of Winneburg stands, midst its own ruins. It has two sets of walls and moats, and must have been quite inaccessible in the old time. It is difficult to get into it now, even without anybody to poke a pike down one's throat, or pour molten lead in your eyes.

Its situation is fine, and from it part of Cochem is seen, and the castle of Cochem, which rises quite close to the town. It is curious how deceptive these places are in size. What seems from below to be a mere fragment of ruin, becomes, at your nearer approach, [211]a most extensive circuit of wall, with many roofless chambers and turrets; just as we never know the size of a tree until it is felled.

The legend of Winneburg, called "the Immured Maiden," merely relates that the master-builder who had contracted to finish the keep within a certain time failed in his contract; and being reproached by his employer, was about to jump into the Moselle from the walls: but a stranger assured him, if he would allow him to build into the wall the little daughter he loved so dearly, he would finish the keep in a day. The rascal consented, and the devil built the little girl up in the foundation of this strong keep-tower.

We doubted the truth of this story, as the master-builder must have been a very active man to have jumped two miles and a half, which is the distance from Winneburg to the Moselle.

Continuing our course from the hill on which Winneburg stands, we enter a narrow part of the valley called the Enterthal. This Enterthal consists of a series of openings in the very high hills; the openings are exquisitely green lawns, surrounded by thick foliage and rock; through or round these openings runs the brook, heaping up stones and spreading into pools, or tumbling down headlong in its hurry to reach its gentle sovereign the Moselle.

The path is rough, and constantly you have to hop from stone to stone across the brook. Thus picking our steps, we came suddenly on a most aristocratic [212]fishing-party, consisting of the burgomaster and his attendants, clad in blue, with red stripes to their caps, and with naked legs. They seemed very successful in procuring trout for the official supper. Their mode of fishing was not scientific or sportsman-like,—an odd-shaped net, which they poked under the banks, being the only tackle of this great man, who did not disdain to wet his own Herr-burgomasterial legs in the pursuit.

After a long ramble an old mill is reached, and a good sketch found; indeed, the whole walk was a sort of diorama of beautiful moving pictures of rock, and tree, and water. The people we met in these valleys were by no means civil; and we found out at last that their incivility was caused by their thinking we were making plans to divert the course of the stream, or otherwise injure their properties.

English ladies were evidently quite new objects of curiosity to the people of Cochem. On leaving the hotel, the ladies of our party immediately became objects to be pointed at, talked about, and stared out of countenance. If the streets had been empty before their appearance, there were always spies of some sort on the alert, who called to doors and windows those who made a perpetual peep-show of these wonderful strangers. Every tea-table and wine-party also, as we were informed, discussed us, and wondered what could induce us to remain at Cochem when we might be enjoying all the gaieties of Trèves or Coblence. Although we passed weeks there their wonder never diminished, nor did their curiosity cease. They [213] seemed to have no idea of scenery being worth anything.

Luckily, this unpleasant curiosity was confined to the people of the town; in the country a hearty "*Guten tag,*" or "*Gute nacht,*" always greeted us, and the greatest readiness to direct or assist us was always shown by the peasants: one man was, it is true, exceedingly tickled at the idea of our asking the way to a valley which we were already in, and could scarcely answer for laughing. Evidently, too, they in general fancied that so important a place as Something-*heim,* or whatever the name of the place happened to be, ought to be well known to every one.

The castle of Cochem affords a most agreeable retirement to those who are fond of reading, sketching, or musing through the summer's day: unlike the ruins on the Rhine, it is wholly uninfested by beggars, donkeys, or venders of faded flowers and wreaths. Here you may walk up the hill and enter by a stone bridge into the outworks; perhaps a few sheep or goats, with an attendant boy, are there: if not, Solitude holds his court amid the deserted walls. Through the ruined window-arches the river is seen, and the town is immediately under us: vines cover one side of the steep hill, and a little chapel nestles itself into a corner where the rock shelters it from stones; above rise the mountains, covered with cherry and other trees to near the top, where young oaks supersede the less hardy fruit-trees: a soft green lawn fills the space surrounded by the outworks of the castle; [214] in the centre stands the massive keep, beside which is a smaller tower, and in the distance, Winneburg is greyly visible.

Cochem was one of the three castles given up to the Countess of Sponheim by Archbishop Baldwin, as a security for the heavy ransom she made him pay: this happened in 1328. About the same period the Jews of Cochem were massacred; the popular fury was raised against them by the story of the supposed murder of the child Werner at Oberwesel on Rhine. The truth appears to be, that the Jews had become richer than the other members of the communities in which they lived, and therefore Envy roused the populace to fury with a fictitious story of murder, and by this means plundered the unfortunate Hebrews, who no longer lived to protect their property.

Cochem suffered terribly when it was taken by Marshal Boufflers, who, after devastating the Palatinate, advanced against this town; thrice his troops were repulsed by the brave defenders, at length the superior numbers of the besiegers forced an entrance, but with a loss of 2500 men, among whom were six colonels: all the inhabitants that remained alive after the pillage were sent into other countries, and only a few ever found their way back. After the taking of the town the cruelties exercised by the French troops were only surpassed by Tilly at Magdebourg.

The assault took place on the fête of St. Louis, [215] and Boufflers sent the news of the taking and burning of Cochem to Louis XIV. as a pleasant gift, well suited to the occasion.

The château of Winneburg was taken and sacked at the same time. This castle afterwards became the family seat of the Metternichs.

For a long time after these outrages, it is said that those who had witnessed the dreadful scenes at the taking of Cochem were wont to start up in their sleep, crying, "The French! the French!"

Passing out of Cochem, as we continue on our flowery path, we find ourselves in the shade of the Kreuzberg mountain: it is covered with vineyards, which produce a small quantity of excellent wine.

The next town is Clotten; between it and Cochem a fine range of rocky precipices form an amphitheatre, that dwarfs even the gigantic works of the old Romans. What ants we appear when from a rock we look down on our human mole-hills!

The church at Clotten is remarkably well placed on an eminence, where its handsome proportions are seen to the greatest effect. The town is very dilapidated and irregularly built: there are some very picturesque houses in it still, but the old walls and gate-towers have nearly all disappeared to make room for the vines.

Clotten Castle.

At a little distance from the town is the ruined tower, that alone survives of the former castle of [216]Clotten; it is partially undermined, and a great hole broken into its centre. The castle of Clotten was extensive, and very strong; at one time it was the residence of a queen, Richenza of Poland. She was the wife of Miceslaus II., and during her husband's lifetime she managed all the affairs of the kingdom: at his death she was made Regent during her young son's minority, but the Poles drove her out of their kingdom, and she took refuge with her son Casimir in Clotten: here she shut herself up, and Casimir became a monk. Some years after, a deputation from Poland waited on Casimir, and begged him to return to Poland as king; this he did, the Pope releasing [217]him from his vows on the whimsical condition that all the Poles of good birth should cut their hair close to the point of the ear, in perpetual recollection of their king having been a monk.

Richenza endeavoured to persuade her son not to accept the throne, but her arguments did not convince him of the vanity of royalty; she remained in this country, constantly residing at Clotten Castle, near which she built a hermitage with a chapel, to which she often retired.

A fine reach of the river is seen from the ruin, and behind it is a deep valley, in which one or two mills are just perceptible through the trees that envelope the course of the brook which turns their great wheels.

The spires of the churches are in general finely pointed, the one at our feet, as we stand here, is a fair example of their style of architecture. On Sundays and fête-days they are crowded; often they are so full, that late-comers are obliged to stand in the doorway or outside: the crowd is made up of both men and women; the head-dresses of the latter are gay and graceful. The embroidered cloth or velvet covering the thick plaits of the unmarried girls, the close caps of the old women, and the smart streaming ribbons of the young wives, make the heads of the crowd like a bed of tulips.

The men always wear blue blouses and black hats, or plain cloth caps, so they are commonplace-looking enough: the boatmen are alone, of their sex, [218]picturesque; a red cap sets them off amazingly, and they seem to have a very good opinion of themselves, if we may judge by the ease with which they joke the *mädchen* they pass on their voyage.

A good many fish are caught in the river, but they are generally small. All day long solitary men sit in boats, and at long intervals dip up and down nets that move on a pole at the end of a swivel: they must have immense patience, and consume, we should suppose, the greater part of their earnings in the tobacco that they constantly smoke. The casting-net also is much used, but then there must be two men, one to pole the boat into the rapids while the other swings in his net.

Fishing.

[219]
[Contents]

CHAPTER XVIII.

From Cochem, an easy walk brings the tourist within reach of no less than seven castles,—viz. Beilstein, Cochem, Winneburg, Clotten, Treis, Elz, and Pyrmont. The first four we have already noticed: in this chapter we will make a walking tour to the other three named.

Leaving Clotten behind us, we walked on, under a broiling sun, to Pommern. At the back of Pommern is a long, winding, narrow valley, through which the Pommerbach runs. Where it enters the Moselle, the banks of our river are covered with turf and shade-spreading trees. Under these latter we lay, enjoying the cool after our hot, dusty walk. The brook was nearly dry, so we made an agreement with a wild-looking girl, who was watching some cows drink in the river, that she should for the sum of twopence sterling fetch us a pannikin of fresh, cold water, we stipulating to look after her cows in the meanwhile. [220] We found our task rather difficult, as the cows were a most unruly set of brutes, who, not recognising our authority, wished to make their way into the adjoining gardens. At length, however, the water arrived, and the bargain was completed.

Most luxurious was the fresh well-water, the tree-shade, and the rest: a cigar also lent its "enchantment to the view," which embraced a reach of the river, with the woods on its shores, glowing in the noonday haze. Close to us was an ancient château, with its high-peaked roof and many gables; a tower was at one end, and over the roof appeared the church spire. The brook trickled past, and the pollard willows on its green banks marked its course down to the river. The château is now only used as a farm, and the upper part was stored with hay. Formerly it was the residence of a knight, who held it in fief from the Archbishop of Trèves.

Our river lay so still, so clear, so blue beneath us; she also seemed resting till the heat should pass. The mountains, towers, and towns were watching as she slept over the glorious beauty of our Fairy Queen Moselle. As of old, in her earliest days, the freshness of purity still was in her waters,—still innocence and beauty were combined in her azure form; but who shall describe the glory of her maturity, the loveliness of her now perfected form?

It was noontide, and no foot was stirring. The birds had ceased their songs, the trees were motionless, and the still mountains were repeated in the [221] stream, as though they had plunged from their burning heights headforemost into the cool wave.

And thus we sat and mused: speech would have been desecration. Peace was on the earth! What sermons Nature preaches!—always eloquent and simple. How she touches our hearts, and teaches us the truth; while human eloquence, with all its art, fails to impress or rouse us from our state of apathy! What lessons may be learnt, what blessings gained, in a summer's ramble by rivers' banks, and through the mighty forest, where the silence is more eloquent than words; or on the mountain-tops, where earth seems already left behind, and the sky appears almost within our reach!

A little below Pommern, where a large island ends, we crossed to Treis, and went through the meadow valley to the base of the rock on which Treis Castle stands. It was a good climb to the summit, and the path appeared as unfrequented as the forest round the princess who slept until an adventurous knight woke her with a kiss.

The castle of Treis belonged to a very ancient family, who sent knights to the Holy Land under Godfrey de Bouillon. Afterwards it passed into the hands of Queen Richenza of Poland, who gave it to the Convent of Brauweiler, and it was henceforth garrisoned for the Church by dependants of the Archbishop of Trèves.

On one occasion, the Pfalz-graf of the Rhine sent word to the Governor of the castle that the Church [222] did not want forts, as it was sufficiently protected by the Divine power. The Governor acquainted the Bishop, and he excommunicated the Pfalz-graf for his impiety (a step the bishops always seem to have taken in their personal quarrels). The Pfalz-graf, however, did not care for the Bishop's threats, and took the castle.

The angry Bishop assembled an army, and marched to retake this Church property. He soon appeared before the castle, and, with his crucifix in his hand, summoned it to surrender, and upbraided the Pfalz-graf for seizing it.

The Pfalz-graf, seeing the army of the Bishop was too numerous for him to contend with successfully, began to think the Bishop's arguments were strong ones, so he quietly gave up the castle.

The poet ends by saying what may be thus almost literally translated:—

"The Cross a perfect victory gained,

"Thus was its mightiness maintained."

This castle is curiously constructed. It is placed on the summit of a neck of land, both sides of which are precipitous. The keep is at the outer extremity of this neck, and the high rock on which it stands towers perpendicularly from the valley to the height of some four hundred feet. The main part of the castle was on the neck of land, and at the inner end of the neck was a very strong gate-tower and other buildings. These three portions of the castle were joined together by strong walls: but if the [223]gate-tower was forced the garrison could first of all defend the centre, which was divided by a great ditch from the gate-tower; and, finally, they could retire into the keep, which formed a castle in itself. Thus the assailants had to take three separate fortresses.

The tower and considerable fragments of the other parts of this castle still remain, wrapped in solitude. The old hall can still be traced. Where the knights caroused and the ladies smiled is now the haunt of the owl, who sleeps among the branches of ivy that are gradually forcing out the stones from the old walls.

IVY-GIRT RUINS.

From the ruined, crumbling wall,
Ancient fragments downwards fall,
No longer held in iron grasp
By ivy hands, which twining clasp
Those ancient towers and turrets grey,
To which their girdling brings decay.
As an old nation, tottering to its fall,
Doth foreign legions to its armies call,
A time triumphant! then the hireling Band,
That erstwhile strengthened, seize on the command.
Alike the ivy and the friend
Their aid insidious freely lend,
And gradual push their fibres in,
Until the tower or land they win,—
Until the yoke is firmly placed,
Or firm the twigs are interlaced;
Then dies all freedom from the conquered land,—
Then is the ancient tower compelled to stand,
Supporting by its strength the plant whose sway,
Like despot monarch's, brings it sure decay.
Years wear away, the despot's crown
Is green with laurel of renown.[224]
In slavery the nation groans:
Griped by the iron twigs, the stones,
Disjointed from their firm array
By tyrant plants' (or monarchs') sway,
Fall crashing down, and in like ruin hurled
Are walls, and stones, and conqu'rors of the world;
Oppressors and oppressed all equal share
The curse inhaled in slavery's foul air.

Treis boasts a fine church and good inns. Carden is a town of size, and many of the buildings deserve notice, the first is the old toll-house, the landing-place.

Toll-house.

72

On the hill opposite Carden is a chapel high upon a rock: the road leading to it has at intervals shrines, at which the religious processions halt on their way to the chapel. Through the vineyards inland of the town there is also a road, with shrines at every ten yards; this likewise leads up to a Calvary chapel. Carden, in the number of its religious edifices, surpasses all the other small towns on the river.

Many of these buildings are now secularised into barns and outhouses, but the church of St. Castor has just been repaired, as also a small, elegant chapel, that stands close to the river.

LEGEND OF ST. CASTOR.

For many years St. Castor lived in the forest, eating nothing but herbs, and drinking only from the clear spring. He taught the Gospel to all, and was much reverenced by his hearers.

The people, who were living in rough huts in the forest, now collected by St. Castor, built a village, and raised a church to the glory of God. His work completed, the Saint died; and in the course of centuries men forgot where his body had been laid, until a certain priest dreamt, and in his dream it was revealed to him where the Saint slept. Thrice this dream was repeated; so, going to the Bishop of Trèves, the priest told him what had occurred. Search was then made, and the bones of the Saint were discovered; and over them was raised the stately church [226] which we see at the present day, and which is dedicated to this good Saint.

Brauer's Inn is good, and Carden is a very interesting old place. The space near the church is surrounded by funny-looking, high-peaked old houses, a group of which we here give.

The highly picturesque and interesting castle of Elz is about four miles distant from Carden. It is situated on a great rock in a narrow valley, and surrounded on three sides by the Elz brook, that nearly encircles the rock. The hills surrounding are higher than the rock the castle is on, and completely shut it in. They are densely covered with forests, full of roe-deer: hares, foxes, and occasionally wolves, are shot there in winter.

The lord of the castle sometimes comes there to shoot, or to fish in the Elz brook, which is swarming with trout.

We slept in Carden, so as to have the whole day [227] to explore the valley of Elz; and early the following morning we set off over the hills, passing out from the town under one of its little old gateways, several of which still remain.

Coming suddenly on Elz as we gained the top of the mountain above it, the view was very striking; we might have been living in the dead centuries, it looked so perfectly habitable; and yet there was such a quaint look about it, it seemed scarcely real. Soon after we met some of the Count's people going out with dogs and guns: they were dressed after the fashion of huntsmen whose representatives appear nowadays only in theatres,—at least, so we thought until now.

On reaching the castle, we found it more ruinous [228] than we at first had supposed. On ringing a bell we were admitted, and shown over the rooms, in which are preserved many old pieces of armour, arms, pictures, and furniture; also spoils of the chase.

The shapes of the rooms, and the staircases leading to them, are wonderful: two American artists were hard at work, sketching interiors and old furniture.

We read of a knight, George of Elz, so far back as the tenth century, figuring at a tournament at Magdebourg; and the family holding this castle were always of the highest consideration. But they appear to have been a very turbulent race, and much given to quarrelling amongst themselves, even on some occasions slaying each other; and a family agreement was signed by three of the brothers, who seem to have all resided at Elz, which concluded with the following extraordinary terms:—"He of us who shall during this peace kill either his brother or son (from which God defend us!) shall be forced to quit the house, and neither he nor his heirs shall have any rights over the castle of Elz, unless expiation for

73

such mortal sin shall be made. He of us who shall disable one of the others, or his wife or child, shall quit the house and never return. He of us who shall wound or stab the other, shall be banished the house for a month."

This wonderful treaty provided that they should assist each other against their common enemies, and they appear to have done so.

Of course, a castle inhabited by such a set of [229]quarrellers is haunted by the ghosts of those murdered; thus Elz is particularly rich in such stories. But, in general, they are only commonplace ghosts,—just ladies knocked into the valley beneath for not kissing an importunate lover, or built into a wall by a jealous husband; or a mournful murderer, who howls through the long winter's nights in expiation of his crimes here committed. In winter time the occupants must need large fires and a good cask of wine to keep out these troublesome spirits. A better one of these ghosts is a lady, who came by her death in the manner recorded in the following version of

THE PERFORATED HARNESS.

The Lady Bertha of Elz was left by her brother, who had gone to fight in the Holy Land, to take care of the castle of Elz; her lover, Count Edmund, had died, and she mourned for him whom she so dearly had loved.

One evening, when the stars were consoling her for the loss of her lover, she sat gazing on them, and tranquillity fell on her heart.

The hours silently passed, and the lady prepared for her rest, little thinking how near to its final repose life was passing. Suddenly she saw glittering of helmets, and heard noises of clanking of armour below in the valley. Rousing her attendants, Bertha armed herself in a light suit of mail, and went forth with her esquires and adherents to oppose the [230]robbers, who came like caitiffs to attack a female by night.

Advancing in front of her friends, the courageous lady addressed the leaders of the marauders, asking why thus they attacked her. An arrow, launched from an unseen bow, pierced her harness: this was the only reply. Bertha fell dying, and her soldiers rushed on and defeated the foe.

The Lady Bertha was laid in a grave near the castle, over which a weeping willow still points out the spot; and in the still, starlight nights, she and her lover, happy in death, sit hand-in-hand, contented and silent.

The castle of Elz was at length taken from its proper possessors by the Archbishop Baldwin of Trèves, who, although outwitted by Lauretta of Sponheim, seems generally to have worsted his enemies.

There had been a long feud between the knights and the Bishop, who at last vowed to reduce them to obedience. He accordingly besieged the castle in form, and, in order to cut off all supplies, caused a new castle to be erected on the rocks opposite (a fragment of it still exists). This new castle he filled with armed men, and at length the knights of Elz agreed to own the warlike Bishop for their liege lord, and henceforth they held the castle as vassals.

Elz.

Three or four miles higher up the valley of Elz is the castle of Pyrmont. It is romantically seated on rocks which border the stream that a little lower [232]down falls in a cascade into a deep pool. This fall is said to have been a favourite resort of the lady whose lover met the sad fate here recorded:—

JUTTA OF PYRMONT.

A minstrel came to the castle-gate,
And tidings ill he bore;
He told of the brave Count Fred'rick's fate,—
The Count was now no more.
For in the far Italian land,
In lowly grave he lay;
Slain by the loathsome headsman's hand,
Though spared in the bloody fray.

74

Of all who loved the noble knight
Only this Page was left,
Who now fulfilled, in woful plight,
His master's last behest;
That he should seek far Pyrmont's walls,
And there his master's fate,
In Lady Jutta's lofty halls,
With speed and truth, relate
How many frays the Count did win
Till that sad field was fought,
Where he and brave Count Conraddin
Both prisoners in were brought;
How then the coward Duke d'Anjou
Struck off his captive's head,
And slew his followers so true
(All save this Page were dead).
The Lady Jutta heard the tale;
No word the lady spake,
But still she sat, and deadly pale,
The whilst her heart did break.

[233]
To convent walls the dying maid
Retired, her days to close;
Soon in the grave her sorrow laid,
God sent her his repose.

Retracing our steps down the valley of the Elzbach, we found a good path leading through the bottom of the vale. Little meadows bordered the brook which we were compelled to cross frequently, but the great stepping-stones afforded a sure footing over the stream in which the trout were greedily rising at flies. It was evening, and on our left the dense foliage was glowing in light, while the meadows and opposite hills were in shade with little puffs of grey spreading in thin lines among the trees.

At the mouth of the valley we came upon Moselkern, and put up at a tidy little inn, where the young lady of the house rather despised two travellers who had no baggage but what their capacious pockets contained. She was a pretty girl, and doubtless a village belle, so had a right to give herself airs. She, however, relented, and became more polite, when we, regardless of expense, ordered the best wine, which cost at least eighteen-pence a bottle.

In all these inns, we observed that the landlord or his representative thought it a matter of necessity to sit and keep company with his guests, even if they did not talk.

Moselkern we found to be a cheerful village, very prettily placed among the trees, just below where the Elz brook falls into the Moselle. Between it and [234] the river is a broad, green piece of land, where boat-building is generally going on.

Here the youth of the place bathe, and the inhabitants meet to discuss the prospects of the coming vintage, and rejoice or mourn over the past one.

There seemed to be a great leaning towards the French on the banks of our river. In most of the villages there is to be found some old soldier, who expatiates to his listeners on the glorious days of the old Napoleon; and many of the better class of villagers speak a sort of mongrel French. Even among the lowest, French expressions are common.

Sketch at Carden.

CHAPTER XIX.

Bischofstein.

Three more castles now claim our attention; they were all places of great importance. Bischofstein appears to have been, as its name denotes, garrisoned for [236] the Bishop (of

75

Trèves), while Thuron and Ehrenburg were held by adherents of the Count Palatine, or other enemies of the Elector of Trèves.

Pursuing our course down the river, we left Moselkern by a path running through gardens, whose hedgerows are vines trained on a lattice-work. We found the peasants digging up fine potatoes, so congratulated them on their crop, and also on the appearance of the grape bunches; but people are never satisfied, and they said, "Yes, it is very good for the wine, and the corn, and potatoes, but the garden greens are all burnt up with the sun:" we thought of the wretched farmer, whose potatoes were all so large there were no little ones for the pigs.

Bischofstein is finely placed on a spur of the rugged mountain; beneath it is a chapel and farmhouse: vines grow in the castle-yard, and wherever a shelf of level ground can be made into soil fit for their cultivation.

There is a great white stripe round the middle of the tower, which the popular belief attributes to a deluge which submerged all the valley, and only stayed its course when half up the tower of this castle; the account given in the following tale is more probable:—

THE BISHOP'S SERMON.

The country round Bischofstein was swarming with robber-knights and pillagers of every degree, to such an extent, that the Archbishop Johann of Trèves sent [237]out a strong band of knights, who took up their abode in the castle of Bischofstein.

The knights stayed the ravages, and soon the robbers found their occupation gone, and good living on plunder a thing of the past; so they took counsel together as to what should be done.

The robbers determined that Bischofstein must be taken and the knights in its garrison slain; therefore, with the utmost secrecy, a plan was concocted by which they succeeded in entering the castle by stealth: thus they were able to seize on the knights and their servants, and they slew every one.

A poor peasant who was in the fort contrived to escape, and he carried the tidings to the Archbishop, who sent out an army, which arrived at the fort and found all the robbers sleeping, quite drunk: these they quickly despatched, and the fort was regarrisoned.

Then the Bishop Johann caused a white line to be made round the wall of the tower, that all rogues should see, and by noting the fate of the robbers preserve themselves from the stern hand of justice. "Thus," said the Bishop, "I preach them a sermon by which evildoers from sin may be saved; if they heed not this warning, the sword must preach in *its* turn."

Hatzeport, which we pass on the way to the castle of Ehrenburg, is a well-built, well-to-do place, with a fine church. It stands at the entrance of one of the innumerable valleys that break the great ridges of mountain that shut in the course of our river.[238]

Crossing from thence to the village of Brodenbach, we enter a gorge of the hills which conducts us to the beautiful valley, at the far end of which the castle of Ehrenburg seems hanging in air.

The contrast of the sweet smiling valley, with its brook murmuring along, makes the stern fortress more gloomy. Leaving the valley, we gradually ascend by a footpath, until at length we reach where the draw-bridge formerly stood; now there is but the stone pillar that used to sustain it.

Some rough steps lead up to the gate-tower, and a ring at the bell brought a chubby-faced child, that looked much out of place amid the ruins. We entered, and an old dreamy man took the place of the child; he led us through a ruined garden that surrounded a tower of immense thickness, entering which he slowly led us by a winding road, that would admit six men to mount abreast, up to the summit of the tower.

To our surprise we now were on a piece of level ground; this tower, which was the only entrance, having been built on a lower ledge of rock.

The garden we were in was neatly kept and full of vegetables; at its extremity stood the castle, from the centre of which, and on a still higher piece of rock, the donjon keep, with its twin towers, rose up: these towers are circular, and joined by a double wall.

76

All round outside the walls was air; the valley seemed far away: for hundreds of feet, a pebble that [239] we dropped fell down, striking nothing till it came into the depths of the valley. Much of the ruin still remains, and the old man showed us how we might ascend to the top of the twin towers.

There we sat wrapped in solitude, the valleys far beneath us, and the hills spread out like a raised map, with here a tint of green where trees should be, and there a grey patch for rock, while over them shone out a bit of molten silver where our river flowed: so was the whole country charted out for us, and here for hours we sat, our senses drinking with delight from the pure well of fresh, sweet pleasure raised by our most novel situation.

The old man sat still beneath us; and the records in our hand told us what the old guide could not, the legends of the place.

The Knights of Ehrenburg were vassals of the great Counts of Sponheim, and very powerful in council and war; the last of the race was Count Frederick, who, according to the Chronicle of Limburg, burnt down a great part of Coblence: his reason for so doing appears in the following legend:—

[Contents]

THE LAST KNIGHT OF EHRENBURG.

Count Frederick of Ehrenburg was the last of his race, his father had died while he was yet young. Feeling his castle to be lonely without a companion, he looked far and near to find a fair lady whom he might love and bring home to be mistress of Ehrenburg.[240]

Having found a suitable lady, he begged her hand from her father, saying that he would give her his castle, his name, and his sword as a dower; but the grim old warrior replied, that though his castle was strong and name great, yet his sword was too bright, too glittering, and new; and added, that his daughter's husband must be able to show some marks of hard fighting on sword or on person. The old warrior further suggested that the young Count should burn Coblence, as he had a feud with that town.

Count Frederick retired and collected his friends, with whom he made many inroads on the burghers of Coblence, and at length he succeeded in burning a part of the town.

He immediately repaired to his loved lady's castle, when, to his great annoyance, he found the fair one was flown. Having heard of her father's wicked promise, that he would give her in marriage when Coblence was burnt, she had retired from the world, and in a nunnery was endeavouring to atone for the crime of her father.

The young Count raged and swore, and eventually took to his bosom a different lady, but no children were granted them, so he was the last of his race.

The records go on to relate how this last Count, having no son of his own, adopted one of the sons of a friend; this boy's name was Walter, and he met with the adventure described in the tale called—[241]

[Contents]

THE TIMELY WARNING.

It was Carnival in Coblence—all the world was there; the streets were thronged with masks, shows and processions were in all the public places; music, dancing, and merriment, reigned supreme.

Walter, the adopted son of the Count of Ehrenburg, longed to visit the gay scene, but the Count had never yet permitted him to go so far away; at length, by dint of importunity, he got leave to set out, but was strongly cautioned to meddle with no one, and avoid all disputes or quarrels: with two stout men-at-arms he went forth.

When arrived at Coblence, he went first to an hotel by the shore; in the windows of this hotel stood the young Count of Isenburg with a beautiful girl, and many of the Count's servants were loitering about the doors of the inn.

The Count of Isenburg, on seeing young Walter, commenced forthwith to mock him, and sneered at the lad's scanty retinue. Walter was angry, but, remembering his promise not to quarrel or fight, strode into the house without saying a word.

Walter had nearly forgotten the incident, and was gazing on the gay crowd that moved to and fro over the old Moselle bridge and in the road under his windows, when a soft low knock came to the door. On opening he found the beautiful girl that he had seen by the side of Count Isenburg; she hastily entered, |242|and said, "Noble youth, you must hasten away, for the Count is now gone into the town to excite the townspeople against you, and unless you depart with great speed, the people, who hate your family, will certainly seize you." She added that, like him she addressed, she did not belong to a noble family, but her father being Count Isenburg's vassal, she was forced to dissimulate and receive his attentions till she could make her escape.

She had scarcely done speaking when the Count appeared in the doorway, his naked sword in his hand, and fury flashing out from his eyes. "What dost thou here, venal wench!" he cried out; "how darest thou speak to this Bastard?" Then, running at Walter, he sought to slay him while off his guard.

But Walter, hastily drawing his sword, not only parried his thrusts, but wounded him sorely; then, whispering adieu to the girl Wallrade, who had given him so kind and timely a warning, he sought out his servants, and rode forth from the town, not without some sharp exchanges of blows between them and the Coblencers, who were collecting in haste to oppose their outgoing.

The Count of Isenburg and a party of citizens followed soon after, and besieged the castle of Ehrenburg; but the garrison mocked them, and when the besiegers retired, they advanced upon Coblence, and burnt down the suburbs.

Walter contrived to rescue from durance the girl Wallrade, who, together with her father, had been |243|thrown into prison; but the chronicle does not relate whether he married his fair preserver or no.

After an afternoon spent at Ehrenburg we returned to the village of Brodenbach, where there are several clean little inns.

The great castle of Thuron well merits its name of "the Throne Castle;" it stands on the heights above Alken, which is a considerable village at a short distance from Brodenbach.

At Alken.

|244|

At Alken, and in the vicinity, many Roman coins, coffins, and pieces of armour, have been found; so it is probably a place of considerable antiquity. It is sheltered by a bold rock that juts into the stream, and was connected with the castle of Thuron by a line of towers, which still remain standing in the surrounding vineyards.

On the preceding page we have given a sketch of one of the little chapels, with a line of shrines on each side of the steps that lead up to it; these shrines and chapels form a leading feature in the Moselle scenery. Nestled under the side of the hill on which the great castle of Thuron stands, this little chapel, with its sharp-pointed spire, is in fine contrast to the huge cliff and massive walls; but there is a look of age about it and the old houses near which renders the whole scene in perfect keeping.

On leaving the river to explore our way up to Thuron, we enter one of those beautiful valleys into which the hills so constantly break; a clear trout-stream runs through it, and the mountains close it in on all sides.

One or two labourers are past, a "good day" exchanged, and then we commence the ascent, which is long and steep. The path lies through a wood, and not a single person did we meet in our walk, after leaving the valley, until on the top of the hill we found some wood-gatherers. Here the castle with its two towers appeared; it is the most stately ruin we ever saw, very extensive, grandly placed, and so inaccessible, |245|that when we arrived at the base of its outer wall we could not get in.

Thuron Castle.

At last we managed to scramble through a window, and then luxuriated in the great ruin; blocks of stone and bushes usurp the ancient place of knights and ladies, and no sound is heard but the song of birds. |246|This castle was built by the Count Palatine Henry, in 1209, after he came back from the Holy Land; he was the delegate of his brother, the Emperor Otho IV., and he exercised a sovereign power over the countries adjoining the

Moselle. He often resided in his new castle, and had many feuds with the Archbishops of Trèves and Cologne, who enjoyed certain rights of sovereignty in Alken.

These discords gave rise to the celebrated siege of Thuron. It is celebrated, not so much for the deeds of valour there carried on, as for the extraordinary quantity of wine there drunk,—no less than three thousand cartloads having been consumed by the besiegers alone.

[Footnote]

SIEGE OF THURON.

The Knight Zorn commanded for the Count Palatine in his strong castle of Thuron, when the Archbishop of Trèves advanced and laid siege to it. The commander of the castle, who was supported by a brave garrison, amply provisioned, laughed the besiegers to scorn.

Finding they made no progress, the Archbishop's Commander sent to the Archbishop of Cologne for assistance. This was willingly granted, and the united armies blockaded the castle. Zorn expected daily that they would deliver an assault, but to his surprise, day after day and night after night went by, and no movement took place in the camps of his enemies; eating and drinking seemed their sole occupation.

Every house in the neighbourhood was ransacked [247] by the troops of the Church, and every cellar was emptied; carts also arrived in long strings, bringing great butts of wine. Thus they went on drinking and singing, while Zorn from above looked on astonished at these most unusual proceedings.

Occasionally a herald arrived, and summoned Zorn to surrender; but no assault was delivered.

The empty casks of the Church were piled up in heaps, and at the end of two years they formed a mass which looked like a great fortress; and a message was sent to the castle, that if the garrison did not surrender they would continue to drink till the whole country was dry, and the empty casks sufficient to form a fortress larger and stronger than Thuron.

Zorn now agreed to capitulate, and at length it was settled, that he and his garrison should retire unmolested, that the soldiers of Cologne should at once leave the country, and that the castle should be dismantled.

One unlucky personage appears to have been excluded from this pacific arrangement: this was a village magistrate, who had acted as spy for the besieged. He was taken by the conquerors, and a rope having been stretched over the ravine, between the castle and the hill of Bleiden, he was suspended at an immense height from the ground.

Another version of this story makes the magistrate-spy to walk across ropes so stretched over the valley; and it is added, that he accomplished the feat, and in gratitude built the chapel which we see (now in ruins) on the hill to the right of the castle. [248]

The views from Thuron are very extensive, a long reach of the river leads the eye back to the villages and cliffs we have past; undisturbed by those infesters of the Rhine, who turn every place of interest on that river into a tea-garden, we can here enjoy our meditations without hindrance, and muse our fill.

THE BIRD AND THE RUIN.

I gazed on an ancient keep;
Its hoary turrets high,
And its gloomy dungeons deep,
Its mould'ring cistern dry,
All seemed to me to say,
"Behold in our decay
"An emblem of mortality!"
Whilst thus I mused and gazed,
A little bird upsprang,
To heaven its voice it raised,
And thus it sweetly sang:
"On earth all creatures die,
"But in the holy sky
"Is love and immortality."

[249]

CHAPTER XX.

Gondorf Castle.

The rock that projects into the river below Alken was formerly a very dangerous point for boats to pass; now, owing to the submerged portions having been blasted, it is no longer regarded with terror: but still we see a saint's image placed in a niche of the rock, so that he may be near if required to render any assistance. The summit of this rock is level, [250] and some hundreds of acres of corn are grown on the curious table-land thus formed.

The road from Alken to Coblence is very indifferent, but not so bad as represented by the coachmen of Coblence. One who drove us told us beforehand, that a short time previous a lawyer going this road was upset, and had not since left his bed; but as we found that the road so abused was perfectly safe if ordinary care was taken, we suspected that, like the man in the play, who wished "every soldier would kill a lawyer and take the legal consequences," the learned gentleman's driver must have had some spite against him. Our driver was a funny fellow, and among other things, speaking of a village we were passing, he said, "They make excellent wine there, although they are Protestants."

At Kür we found so clean and pleasant an inn, that we stopped for the night. As we were resting at one of the open windows, through which the still evening was visible, suddenly the shutters flapped to, and in an instant the water was ruffled, the wind howling, and everything creaking and slamming.

The storm grew louder and fiercer, the waters were boiling: then came a crash through the hills, as if the mountains were rent; the rain poured in jets from the sky, the blackness of which was illumined by lightning, which at short intervals flashed over the valley.

Soon the storm had passed by, and the ever calm moon was floating serenely in heaven. [251]

The lights of the stars fell tremulously down on the still agitated waters. The air was so sweetly refreshing, that we sat on and on enjoying the now lovely evening, till we were quite startled by being suddenly summoned to supper,—not exactly startled at the notion of supper, but astonished to see the ghost of a first-rate-inn waiter, for such our summoner seemed, clad, not in grave-clothes, but clothes of grave hue, and a white handkerchief, folded with the greatest precision, round his waitership's neck. We had so long been absent from civilisation, that we were rather abashed at so fine a gentleman waiting on us rugged wayfarers, as we appeared; so we came quietly up to our table, modestly ate, and retired to our rooms.

In the morning, to our relief, we found our stately waiter in his shirt-sleeves and not very dandy continuations; so we mustered up courage to settle our bill, and departed, to revel among uncivilised castles.

Kür was formerly a domain belonging to the Archbishop Poppo. He gave it to the ecclesiastics of the Cathedral at Trèves, and the wine there produced—which was more than sixty tons annually—was used by the recipients as table-wine, the surplus serving to pay for its transport: thus they drank their wine at no cost. The Bishop, in presenting this gift, told the clergy, "that he hoped to have their prayers at the last judgment." In 1802 the vineyard was sold, and a Jew who bought it bequeathed it to the civil [252] hospital at Coblence; and "thus," adds the writer we quote, "the Israelite nobly revenged his race on the Archbishop Poppo, who was described in a document of the period as a friend of Christians and a mortal enemy of Jews."

Traversing a green bank of turf, we arrive in ten minutes at Niederfells. On the opposite side of the river is Gondorf, and a farthing ferry deposits us under the walls of the old Stammschloss, or family house, of the Counts von der Leyen, given at the head of the chapter.

Lower Castle at Gondorf.

80

Members of this family have figured in history as generals in the Imperial armies, in the Swedish, French, and Turkish wars; and as deans and prebends in the Rhenish churches and chapters.

The last of this time-honoured race, the Count Philip, died in 1830 at Cologne. He was buried, in accordance with his expressed desire, in the little [253]churchyard above the castle of Gondorf, where his bones lie in the midst of a people to whom his forefathers and he had endeared themselves by centuries of charity and kindness.

The motto of this family was, "Rock I am; on rock the lily never thrives, for in rock-clefts the eagle only lives."

THE RED SLEEVE.

The Chronicle of Gondorf tells us, that in the olden times the judges of Gondorf used to wear red robes when pronouncing sentence of death on criminals; and the citizens regarded these robes with great veneration, considering them to be part and parcel of their own dignity.

So exemplary were the inhabitants in their behaviour, that many years passed without the robes being wanted; but at length a criminal was brought before the Court, and found guilty.

The attendants searched and the judges searched, but no red robes could be found: time and moths had consumed them, all but one sleeve. The situation was difficult, for the people would not believe that justice was done unless they saw the red robes.

A happy thought lit up the face of one Judge, and this was his plan: each Judge in his turn was to put on the one sleeve, and presenting himself at the window there deliver his judgment, hiding thus [254]the unrobed part of his person. The idea was deemed a hit, and put into practice accordingly,—the populace being led to believe that the Judges gave their opinions thus separately, in order that the opinion of one should not bias the minds of the others. It is added, that the people were very much pleased at the whole proceeding; but the narrator does not say what the criminal thought of it, or whether his counsel raised any objection to the irregularity, if not illegality, of a sentence so pronounced.

The lower castle of Gondorf is used as a barn, and looks very dilapidated.

Getting near Cobern, an opening in the trees shows us the castles that crown the hill over the town. A chapel is in the foreground, and here once lived

THE HERMIT OF COBERN.

Robin of Cobern had a beautiful daughter named Else. Her heart had long been given to the Knight Hans of Sable, but Hans had offended the Bishop of Trèves, and so was outlawed and excommunicated.

Hans was obliged to conceal himself, and hastily flying, took refuge for a long while in solitudes. At length he could no longer endure being absent from his beloved, so he procured a harp, and set out for the castle of Cobern, where some festival was then being held. In his character of Minstrel he was [255]readily admitted into the castle, and there he sang a favourite song which Else knew well. The tide of long-past events rushed so tumultuously back upon fair Else's mind that she fainted: when she recovered, the Minstrel was gone. Knowing the hopelessness of his passion, yet unable to conquer it, he now assumed the habit of a Hermit, and established himself where he could sometimes see Else as she rode forth on her palfrey.

One evening the Hermit was sitting silently dreaming of days of happiness, that might have been his in reality, had not his headstrong will marred his prospects. As thus he sat musing, some robbers drew near, and not being aware of the Hermit's proximity, one of them said, "Well, be it so; at midnight we meet: the postern gate is secured, and Else shall be our prize." The robbers were now out of hearing.

The Hermit, who had little doubt of the meaning of the few words he had heard, hastened up to the castle in order to warn the Count Robin. At midnight the robbers came on, and it then was found out that the postern gate yielded at once to their efforts, which showed that some treachery was working within; but, spite of both force and fraud, the robbers were beaten. The Hermit, fighting most valiantly, fell mortally wounded, and when the fight ended his life was fast ebbing. The Knight and his daughter stood by him; to the Knight's eyes the valiant Hermit was dying, but Else wept for her lover.[256]

In his hour of death concealment was no longer necessary; and Hans avowed his identity, and begged that his body might be laid in the chapel below in the valley, that so in death he should still be near his loved Else.

Then turning his eyes upon her, who, whatever his faults, had but one feeling for him that had so long and faithfully loved her, he said, "Farewell, my beloved; in heaven I trust we may meet!"

The town of Cobern lies at the foot of a lofty hill, which separates two valleys that meet in a level plain close to our river. This town was strongly fortified and defended by the castles, of which the lower one still exists, and is shown in the vignette on the opposite page. The drawing is taken from the wall of the upper castle, of which only one tower and a very few fragments remain.

In the upper castle-yard also stands an elegant chapel; it is hexagonal, and supported inside by a cluster of pillars, which spring from the centre, from these start six pointed arches: the interior is chaste.

This chapel is called by the people the Church of the Templars, because the castle, in whose walls it stands, was inhabited by some of the Knights of the Temple after the suppression of their Order. The proper name of the building is the St. Matthias Chapel, and it was the principal station of the great pilgrimage which yearly took place from Coblence to Trèves. [257] These processions now are less frequent, but still, in a modified form, they often take place.

With song and banners waving, these processions wind their way along, stopping at intervals when before a shrine. The background is formed by ruined [258] castles, woods, and vineyards; the songs resound among the hills as in the old days of Germany, when churches there were none, and God was worshipped under the holy vault of heaven; where the visible beauties of his works preached the religion of Nature to those who had not yet heard Christ's Gospel. Sorrow it is, and shame, that so much mummery should now be mixed with that which was so clear and simple when proceeding from His lips.

A legend of Cobern, relating to the old possessors of the castle, which still stands, is called

[Contents]

THE CHARACTERISTIC MARK OF COBERN.

The battle was won, the enemy defeated and flying, when the Commander of the army collected his forces and caused proclamation to be made that the young warrior of Cobern, who had saved his life at the risk of his own, should stand forth. For a long time no one came forward, the modest soldier not wishing to make too great a service of what he had done.

At length a young man advanced and said he was the man, whereon all hastened to praise him, and the Commander offered his thanks and bade him kneel down to be knighted. Then out stepped the true man of Cobern, and addressed the young man thus: "Of Cobern thou sayest thou art, O Goliath! then tell to this gallant assembly, what is the sacred and characteristic mark of that place?"

The impostor not being of Cobern, was unable to [259] answer the question; he stuttered and turned pale, whereon the Commander ordered him to be placed in fetters.

Then the true Coberner said, the secret mark, only known to our townspeople, is this: "Beneath the high altar in the Church of Cobern is a spring; this spring bubbles and murmurs while the priest prays."

The brave man, whose modesty was highly extolled, was knighted in place of the young man who had tried to assume a credit not due to him; and the Knight so made was the first lord of the Castle of Cobern, and for centuries his family flourished there.

Among his descendants were three sisters, so renowned for their beauty that they were called "The beautiful Trefoil of Cobern."

82

Cobern was the country of the poet Reiff, whose sonnets, of a *triste* character, were much prized. The ruins which cover the country are said to have much influenced, and given this sombre character to, his writings.

The earliest traditions of this town record that a certain Lubentius, who was a contemporary of St. Castor of Carden, converted the ancient inhabitants and performed many miracles; and on one occasion a dispute having arisen between the canon, Peter of Carden, and the chaplain, William of Cobern, as to the respective merits of their two patrons, they fought it out with their fists. William of Cobern being the biggest and strongest, his cause was the best; so Saint Castor must rank after Lubentius.[26]

On the fête of Lubentius fires were lighted on the surrounding hills, in emblem of the light of the Gospel, which dispersed the darkness of Paganism.

This fête took place at the time of the vintage, and the assisters thereat frequently imitated their champion, William the Chaplain, and strove to uphold their patron's authority by the same arguments, the new wine giving life to old quarrels.

The ancient documents relating to Cobern are filled with histories of the quarrels of the inhabitants one with another, or with those of the neighbouring places.

The last Knight of Cobern was Johann Lutter, who, being taken prisoner by the citizens of Coblence, was by them beheaded as a disturber of the public peace.

St. Matthias Capelle.

[261]
[Contents]

CHAPTER XXI.

Winter Scene.

Autumn had long been turning the green leaves to gold. A tinge of yellow first appeared upon the trees; then warmer and brighter grew the foliage; the vintage came and ended; the corn-harvest was long stored away, and, like the Roman Empire, more gorgeous in decay than in its prime. The forest stood crowned with a thousand hues,—crowned like a sacrifice of old [262] prepared for death,—prepared to offer up at Nature's shrine the loveliness she gave.

The most gorgeous of the seasons, Autumn is still the saddest. We look on the fallen leaves and think of friends departed; the useless heaps that lie around the stems remind us of our lost time, and as the winter comes age seems stealing on our brows. Who can say, I shall see spring again? Yet the lesson thus taught us is for our good. Time moves on and brings us to eternity; therefore, is it not well for man that Nature warns him of the lapse of Time?

Nor is winter to us an unpleasant or unprofitable period. In winter we meet again our friends, we gather round our hearths, or meet by theirs those that we love; old friendships are renewed, old ties are strengthened, and by the cheerful fireside we repeat tales of old times,—tales of days that made our country famous; in gaining which fame our fathers bled, and we their descendants receive fresh strength to emulate their deeds.

In the old days, upon our river's bank, the Germans deemed Christmas more sacred than all other times; for then, they said, "The gods walked upon the earth."

So should it be. At Christmas, we should with the old year bury our quarrels and our cares; and as our religion teaches, look forward with a sure hope and certain faith to the new year, which assuredly will dawn.

In the dark days of Paganism we can well imagine [263] how men's minds were affected with the gloom of impending winter; but we are no longer fearful of the coming time, now that we know eternity is open and that we shall live hereafter.

THE SUCCESSION OF THE SEASONS.

The day succeeded night, and eve the morn,
In those far ages back ere Man was born;
Then only Elves and Fairies played
Beneath the leafy covert's shade,
And all was Summer, and the bright sun shone
On this fair world, and ruled it for his own;

83

For Winter there was none, nor cold
Nor cloud in those bright days of old.
The birds and flowers for ever bloomed and sang,
The springs perpetual from the dark rock sprang;
Time strode with even step along,
His path begirt with flowers and song.
The dainty Elves and Fairies wandered free,
Passing their hours in mirth and harmless glee,
Until at length of sunshine they
Grow weary, and for some new thing pray.
Then Autumn first into the world was sent,
And all the Elves and Fairies were content;
But soon they learnt that, Change begun,
Its onward course would ever run.
Succeeding Autumn, cold, dark, Winter's reign
Commenced; the Elves wished Summer back again,
Fearing no more its light to see,
Dreading lest thus Eternity
Should Time have swallowed up, and, falling fast,
Their fairy tears were shed for pleasure past,
As ours too often vainly fall,
Seeking our lost ones to recall;

[264]

Till Spring the wintry earth revived again,
Refreshing all things with its gentle rain.
Then danced the Elves, then sang the Fairies gay,
And so the winter clouds all passed away;
Henceforth the seasons in succession rolled,
And new years hastened to supplant the old.

Thus let us learn when coldest winter chills,
And darkest night with fear our bosom fills,
To trust in His unfailing love, and turn
Our hearts to where, with thankfulness, we learn
That, as the Spring and Summer cold succeed,
And morning to the night,
So will His mercy wandering footsteps lead
From darkness into light.

Between Cobern and Winningen our river makes its last great bend at a point where a splendid mass of rock towers up on the left bank. It is the last of the Eifel family of Giants we encounter; for, beyond Winningen, the scenery on that side becomes softer in character, smaller hills become undulations, and then, as we get close to Coblence, these slope into the garden with which the plain is covered.

The first cluster of houses we encounter after leaving Cobern is Dieblich. It lies quite back from the stream, and looks anything but a place that would be especially selected by witches to carry on their spells and incantations; yet so infected (say the Chronicles) was this town with witches, that in a short time twenty-five individuals were burnt there, who all confessed that they were in the habit of meeting on a neighbouring [265] mountain and worshipping a goat, who was an incarnation of the Evil One.

They also confessed to having emptied cellars, cursed cattle, raised storms, destroyed the harvests, and performed all the feats usually attributed to those unfortunates. The key to the true causes of their being persecuted lies, perhaps, in the following tale, which, if true, clears the memory of one witch of Dieblich. Spite, envy, jealousy, or some other evil passion being, in all probability, the denouncer of the unfortunate witches in nine cases out of ten.

[Contents]

THE FATE OF THE FALSE SWEARER.

84

An old country Squire who was unmarried, having been much struck with the appearance of a young girl of Dieblich, determined to ask her mother to give him the daughter in marriage; so he donned his best suit and set off.

Now Elsbeth was, as she richly deserved, the belle of the place. Many and many a head had been broken, and many a tall wine-bottle emptied, in honour of her. The mother was naturally proud of her daughter's attractions; indeed, perhaps, as mothers will do, she rather overrated her merits.

When the Squire rode up to her door, the housewifely frau was busy preparing the soup, which forms so essential an item of dinner in Germany. "Good day! God be with you!" said he. "And with you also, mein Herr!" replied she; "what brings your [266] honourable and ever-to-be-delighted-in presence to the door of my humble abode?"

Then followed the explanation of how the Squire would honour the buxom Elsbeth by making her his wife; but the frau, nettled at the Squire's manner, demurred,—thinking much greater ceremony should have been observed in asking the hand of the Belle of Dieblich.

The Squire, not expecting any obstacle, was astonished, then angry; but at that moment the Beauty entered, and he addressed himself for an answer to her. She laughed in his face, and averred that he had better marry her mother; so off rode the Squire, vowing vengeance.

It was, however, a very dear joke for the mother; the Squire hurried off to Coblence, and there denounced her for a witch. Her friends and her daughter's lovers came forward to plead in her favour, and swore that she was a godly old woman, who never had harmed man or beast.

The false-swearing Squire swore to the contrary, and said these neighbours of hers were bewitched. The Court, of course believing a rich man rather than a number of poor ones, ordered the old woman to be put to the rack; there she confessed sins of which she had never been guilty, and then she was burnt.

Elsbeth, afraid she should meet the same fate, jumped into the river.

The wicked Squire rode thoughtfully home, beginning to fear that he had not gained peace of mind, [267] though he had had his revenge. He came in sight of his house, and perceiving a storm was arising, pushed on with all haste; but it is in vain to fly from our fate: the lightning flashed out, and his horse starting, reared,—then bounding forward, it hurled its rider with force to the ground. Thus perished the swearer of lies.

At Winningen the inhabitants are Protestants, and are, says M. de Bourdelois, "distinguished for their religion, language, and manners, above their Romanist brethren." The vine is nearly the sole object of culture. Formerly, at Pentecost, a very great fête was held in the neighbouring forest, at which was collected all the nobles and knights, burgomasters and aldermen, of the district; the Lord of Elz gave a huge tun of wine, and the monasteries of St. Martin and Marienrod sent the eatables, to this gigantic pic-nic.

The people living at this part of our river, especially a little lower down, near Lay, have been subject to terrible disasters, caused by the ice which collects here in winter, and then, suddenly breaking up, floods the whole country. In 1670 the Lahn, being unfrozen, and swollen with the rain that had fallen in the Taunus range, rushed down, and sweeping past Coblence, forced its way up the Moselle; thus causing great icebergs to form in our river, which killed the vines and swept away orchards, houses, men, beasts, and boats, all in one chaos of general destruction. In 1709, thrice the ice became melted and then froze again, each time [268] spreading disaster abroad; Coblence, Güls, Lay, and Moselweiss, all severely felt the effects.

On the hills above Lay is the great drill-ground of Coblence; here the large body of forces collected in Ehrenbreitstein and Coblence are manœuvred. From these heights, too, a remarkable view of the windings of both Rhine and Moselle may be seen. Stoltzenfels and Lahneck appear in the distance. Coblence, with long lines of trees approaching it from all quarters, is just underneath the end of this promontory of rock; the stone bridge of the

Moselle and the boat-bridge of the Rhine are observed; and the strong fortress of Ehrenbreitstein is on the opposite side of the Rhine.

Just opposite to Güls the Hunsruck mountains recede inland from the Moselle, and our glad river flows now through a plain. Her course is nearly finished, her journey is almost accomplished; soon she will unite her pure spirit and her being with the lordly Rhine. But one other city standing on her banks has yet to be described; one other chapter is required to finish the life of our sweet river.

CHAPTER XXII.

Coblence is situated at the extremity of a level plain watered by the Moselle and Rhine. It is placed in the angle formed by the junction of those two rivers. Immediately opposite to the town is the strong fortress of Ehrenbreitstein, which has the reputation of being impregnable: it is much doubted whether this fortress would be found as strong as it is represented to be, [270] now the art of gunnery has been so much improved; yet it would certainly be a formidable obstacle to an attacking army. Coblence itself is strongly fortified, and, together with Ehrenbreitstein, is garrisoned by about 4000 men. Every year troops are gathered from other garrisons to the neighbourhood of Coblence, where they encamp and rehearse all sorts of field evolutions.

During the earliest period of the Roman Empire a castle was built by the Romans at the confluence of the Rhine and Moselle. This fortress fell into the hands of the Franks towards the end of the fifth century. Gradually a town arose round the fortress, till the space between the rivers was filled; then two suburbs were built, one called Thal Coblenz, or Coblence in the Valley—this was on the right bank of the Rhine; the other, on the left bank of the Moselle, was called Klein (little) Coblenz.

After a time the town passed into the possession of the Electors of Trèves, and they built a palace and fortified it.

The bridge over the Moselle is of Roman origin; but it has frequently been repaired and partially rebuilt, being subject to great pressure from the breaking up of the ice on the Moselle, when parts of Coblence are frequently inundated.

Ehrenbreitstein is built on the site of an ancient Roman tower, which is described in old maps as *"Turris adversus Germaniam Magnam."* The Archbishops of Trèves built a palace under the walls of this [271] castle, which was by that time much enlarged and strengthened. The palace still remains.

During the Thirty Years' War, the garrison of Ehrenbreitstein was reduced to such straits for provisions, that on one occasion, at a banquet given by the General Commanding to his officers, there were served up to table sixteen mules, eight dogs, and eighty rats,—the latter delicate animals costing twenty sous each: in addition to these appetising viands, a morsel of bread was served out to each guest, the flour to make which cost one hundred florins a bushel.

At the French Revolution, Coblence became the capital of the Department of the Rhine and Moselle; in 1814 it was given to Prussia, and is now the capital of the Rhenish Provinces of Prussia, and the seat of the Government of those Provinces.

Old Coblence was built along the right bank of the Moselle; and its formerly important suburb of Little Coblence formed with it one town, immediately connected by the bridge. This bridge was entirely rebuilt by the celebrated Elector Baldwin of Trèves. It is recorded of him, that he, by his influence, procured the election of his brother Henry to the Imperial throne; and after his brother's death he placed the crown on the head of the Duke of Bavaria: his nephew also was raised to the throne of Bohemia. He travelled into Italy with the Emperor, and was on that occasion surrounded by all the chivalry of the Moselle, the Counts of Elz, Von der Leyen, &c. &c.; in short, he seems to have equalled in power and magnificence any prince [272] of the age. Yet he was outwitted by Lauretta of Sponheim.

The bridge was formerly the great centre of gaiety, and the place most resorted to for exercise and fresh air. Here, on the first day of the new year, came the chief magistrate to receive tribute from the different communities that owed him allegiance. The Seigneurs presented cheeses or a couple of fowls; the Religieuses of Oberwerth a cake, and those of the Chartreuse a quarter of a hundred of eggs.

On the occasion of this ceremony the senators and magistrates were allowed to snowball each other; but the bailiffs of the Elector were not permitted to take a part in this exercise.

A reunion of the authorities also took place on the bridge on the eve of St. Walpurgis. Then the two burgomasters of Coblence and Little Coblence arrived, each with a bouquet of lilies freshly gathered. Lavender and thyme that had been plucked in the woods near Coblence were also made into bouquets and presented to the wives and daughters of the principal citizens.

The Walpurgis eve was, according to the old stories, the great day when the witches assembled from all parts, and rode abroad on the wind, or else bestrode their housewifely brooms. On one of the annual reunions upon the bridge a handsome and well-dressed cavalier, holding a bouquet of the fairest flowers in his hand, was seen wending his way through the crowd. The eyes of all the young maidens were turned with [225] admiring glances upon the cavalier's handsome face, and great was the jealousy when he stopped before Lieschen, and presented his bouquet to her. The plaited tails of their hair became more and more agitated, and meaning looks were exchanged as Lieschen (who, the men said, was lovely, but who, the girls said, was an impudent thing) was led by the hand through the crowd, her conductor being the handsome young stranger; but all their jealousy turned into pity when, the next morning, it was found that Lieschen had vanished. Doubtless the young man was a spirit of evil, who had carried her off to destruction.

On the day of the dedication of the Church all the young people danced on the bridge.

The air inhaled on this bridge was held to be of peculiar salubrity, and an old locksmith, who lived to the age of 120, considered that the length of his life was entirely owing to his daily walk on the bridge; and he believed that he might have lived to a much greater age had not he been prevented one day from taking his accustomed exercise.

[Contents]

LEGEND OF THE MOSELLE BRIDGE.

A youth stood leaning on the parapet of the Moselle Bridge. He thought of the numerous stories then rife in those regions, in which water-spirits played so conspicuous a part. As he silently gazed, and his young heart yearned for something to love—something more [226] pure and ethereal than the Sannchens and Lisbeths of every-day life, a gentle Spirit arose from the waters—a Spirit of purity raised by the Spirit of Love.

"Dreamer," said the pure Spirit of Water, "day after day and night after night I hear thy sighs and complaints. Thy tears fall down into the stream, and cause me to pity thee. Nay more, I could love thy sad heart were I a mortal; but, unlike thee, my poor youth, I live for ever. I was old when thy fathers were young, and young shall I be when thou art departed."

Then broke forth the youth:—"Ever young, ever glorious art thou! Receive but my love, and I shall be contented to pass from my mortal existence at once."

"Nay," gravely replied the pure Spirit, "thou thinkest alone of thy love and thy pleasure; know this for thy good,—all like thee of mortal race must perform the duties of their lives before their great reward is gained. If then thou truly lovest me, and earnestly fulfillest the work appointed thee to do, faithfully and steadfastly pursuing the straight path in life, then will I, when thy years are full, receive thee in my arms, for so only canst thou gain perpetual youth and be a fit associate for even such as I, who am but a handmaiden of the Queen Moselle, who herself is but one of the lesser Spirits of the Universe. Go, and be just, and honourable, and brave; be kind to all, and liberal to the poor; so shalt thou gain immortal youth and me."[227]

The Spirit was gone, and the bright waves shone in the moonlight; the youth returned, silent and thoughtful, towards the city.

* * *

87

Year after year went by, and every night a solitary figure appeared at the same spot on the bridge, until the snows of a century crowned the brows of him who was still in heart but a youth; then his radiant bride appeared, and the pure-hearted man was wafted away on the bosom of the pure Water Spirit.

Still on the waters live spirits, beautiful and pure as that which appeared to the youth, but as yet no other mortal has been found who, at his death, could claim by his own spotless life an immortal bride. And if it is the case that scarce one is sinless enough to claim even a handmaiden among spirits, who shall take his place with those higher hosts that fill the sky? Who shall dare aspire to the central heaven itself?

The Germans of the present time are quite as much given to amusement as their forefathers were; on every possible occasion they indulge in pic-nics, dances, fairs, processions, and festivals of all sorts. Christmas and New-year's Days are perhaps the greatest holidays in the year, but Carnival time is also universally kept as a fête, the same as in Italy.

In summer, excursions into the country are the most favourite amusements; people of all classes, [270] high and low alike, indulge in these excursions. Some of the villages on the Moselle are particularly frequented by the people of Coblence. Güls, Moselweiss, and Lay are often crowded with pleasure-seekers of the poorer class, while the richer are met with at much greater distances; crowned with wreaths, and laughing and singing, these latter seem to pass very merry days in the woods, exploring old castles, &c. Certainly our pic-nics in England are but dull affairs in comparison, but then our belles are on such occasions better dressed, and it might hurt their fine clothes if they went romping about as the German girls do; besides, the impropriety would be shocking.

Coblence is, on the whole, an uninteresting town; it has all the disadvantage of being a garrison without any particular redeeming point; the rivers are quite shut out from the town by the fortifications, and can only be seen by going on to the bridges: however, the hotels, which are very good, command views of the Rhine from their windows; and the Belle Vue may be especially mentioned, as affording most animated scenes to those who occupy its apartments, it being just opposite to the bridge of boats, where promenaders sun themselves and military are always crossing and recrossing.

Occasionally the bridge of boats is opened, and steamers, each tugging a fleet of from two to six, or even seven vessels, beat up the stream; or else a gigantic floating village of wood comes gliding down, quite filling the aperture, and looking as if it would [271] carry away the whole bridge. It is wonderful the skill with which these unwieldy rafts are managed.

In the town there are good shops, but not much outward display; and though, as we have mentioned, not in itself very interesting, yet there are many and beautiful excursions to be made from it: the society is said to be agreeable.

Near the junction of the rivers is the church of Saint Castor; it stands in a large open space, and is a stately and interesting building: it contains a handsome monument to one of the Electors of Trèves.

The palace is a large house, not remarkable in any way; in it is a chapel where English service is performed, as there are a good many English constantly residing here, as well as the swarms of summer visitors. Most of the more important buildings are near the Moselle Bridge, or between it and the church of Saint Castor; that is to say, they are in the old part of the town.

Near the Castor Church, in the large square, is the monument erected by the French to commemorate their invasion of Russia. To the inscription recording the object of raising the monument, the Russian General who in his turn invaded the Rhine provinces, added—

"Vu et approuvé par nous,
Commandant Russe de la Ville de Coblence.

"Janvier 1er, 1814."

The monument is a remarkably ugly lump of stone, which perhaps was meant for a fountain, but there is no water. [272]

Very few historical associations belong to Coblence, and those that do are not particularly interesting, so we will turn back to the legends.

LEGEND OF MARIAHILF.1

Near the Moselle Bridge stood a chapel, piously dedicated to the Mother of God and her Son. Within the chapel were images of both Mother and Son.

Here resorted many pilgrims, especially those who suffered under bodily infirmities: among others came a certain man who was paralytic, and given over to death by his physicians. With great labour and trouble he contrived to totter into the chapel by the aid of his staff.

The pilgrims were singing a hymn, in which the words, "Help us, Maria," occurred frequently. The poor cripple endeavoured to join in the hymn, but could not, he was so weak.

At last he made a great effort, and the words from his lips were scarcely audible, but immediately he was relieved: his voice returned to him, and his limbs became strong again; so that he no longer needed his staff, which he *therefore* presented to the chapel.

SAINT RITZA.

Ritza lived in Little Coblence, just opposite to the Church of St. Castor. When the bells tolled for morning prayers she used to walk over the waters to attend at the service, returning by the same road.

One day the waves were high, and the sky full of storms; she hesitated, and finally gathered a vine-branch, with which she endeavoured to assist her tottering steps: but faith had deserted her, and she sank deeper and deeper into the waves—the prop was utterly useless; then she thought on her Saviour and prayed for assistance; instantly she rose again from the waters, and, casting away the false prop, gained the opposite shore.

After her death Ritza was canonised, and her bones were laid in the Church of St. Castor.

Another legend also relates how prayer saved those who had faith. It was on the occasion of a great flood, which submerged a large portion of the town, the people prayed at a shrine and the waters dispersed; then on the sands, by the bridge, a figure was found, which all declared to be the Virgin: it was taken up, and with great pomp placed in a chapel. In after days this image was again thrown into the water by the enemies of Coblence, but again it was washed on to the shore; and, according to the legend, it is now placed near the harbour, where it watches over the safety of the good city of Coblence.

The other stories of Coblence are of a more material character. One tells us of

CORPORAL SPOHN.

The great Corporal Spohn is still well remembered in Coblence; he was one of the most faithful of men. He saved the life of the Emperor Napoleon at the battle of the three Emperors. Napoleon had advanced too boldly, and was in imminent danger of being taken prisoner by the Cossacks; if not, which was more likely still, killed by those wild soldiers. Corporal Spohn having noticed the desperate position of Napoleon, ran up, and an agreement was hastily made, by which Spohn mounted the white horse of Napoleon, who escaped then unnoticed.

The Emperor was saved as a corporal; and the Corporal died as an emperor.

Ever since Spohn has been called the Great Corporal, and Napoleon the Little Corporal.

HENRY AND BERTHA.

Henry was expecting his dearly beloved Bertha to arrive at Coblence; he, therefore, stood watching most anxiously on the old bridge over the Moselle. At last the boat which contained her came into view, and she waved her kerchief to her constant lover.

Alas! before he could clasp her the boat overturned, and Bertha was struggling beneath an arch of the bridge. Henry rushed down to save her, but just as he arrived at the edge of the water she uttered his name and went down.

Marking the place, Henry dashed in and seized on her loosened hair, which floated on the surface of the agitated river: thus he succeeded in saving her life, and gaining from the stream a loving wife.[281]

One more tale we found under the head of "Legends of Coblence," so we conclude the scene therein depicted took place at this town; it is called

THE POET'S DEATHBED.

Max of Schenkendorf is well known in Germany by his songs on those combats for liberty, of which so many took place in his Fatherland. The Poet was in the last stage of consumption.

It was the morning of his birthday. Max lay sleeping in bed, but his wife had arisen, and was now busy adorning his chamber with flowers in honour of the Poet's birthday.

Having arranged all the bouquets, she made up a garland of evergreens, which she placed softly on the brow of the sleeper, fervently praying that it might become an emblem of new laurels which her husband should gain in this new year of his life.

As she leant over him to place the wreath on his head, she tenderly kissed the lips of the sleeper, and softly she murmured, "Oh, would I could kiss you to health!"

The decorations now were completed, and softly the wife stept from the husband's bedside, softly she passed from the chamber.

But as she went out an unbidden guest entered there—Death came over the threshold and took the wife's place. Death strode up to the bed and laid his chill hand on the feverish brow of the sleeper: closer [282]and closer then wound those arms which supplanted for ever those of the wife—closer and closer, until icy and rigid became the frame of the Poet.

An hour slowly passed, and the fond wife re-entered. Max now was lying a corpse, crowned with the wreath that she had placed upon his living brow. In agony she cried, "Wake, O wake, my own, my beloved! Depart not from her who lives but in thee! One word, but one——"

The smile was on his lips, but the spirit was gone, leaving only its imprint on the cold clay.

* * *

"Weep, not, O woman!" said his spirit to her, "weep not for the clay that lies here; the shackles are broken; what earth could not hold, nor love longer detain, can neither be fettered by Death: the body is dead, but the soul lives for ever; it lives in thy love and thy heart; it lives in the sky."

This is the last of our legends; and with a few remarks on the habits and customs of the part of Germany near our river we will come to the conclusion of our last chapter. Not without regret shall we end; for it is a pleasant task, in these cold short days of winter, to record that which brings to our remembrance the long bright days of summer; especially as that summer was spent among such lovely scenes.

The Germans bear the character of being an honest, hardworking, intelligent people, very domestic in their habits, even to exclusiveness; the different classes [283]assort together less than they do in England, but passing communication is freer and less constrained.

During the many weeks we passed on the Moselle, and in a former excursion on our river, we never once encountered a family of tourists of the upper class of Germans. At Bad Bertrich there were some, but they were there because it is a watering-place—not because it is beautiful; and as soon as the season was over away they all went, as if they were afraid to remain at a Bad out of the fashionable season, although the weather was much more suitable for country pursuits than it had been during the season.

This same fashion arrays the dumpy young ladies of Germany in a most strange deformity of inflated petticoats. Bad enough as these things are in England and France, in Germany they are much worse.

The gentlemen are, in general, agreeable, and more truly polite than the French; but French ladies certainly have the advantage over their sisters in Germany.

The poorer classes still bear the stamp of the old German character. They are frugal, hard-working, honest, and cheerful. They are well-mannered and well-informed for their class. They also exhibit considerable neatness and taste in their dress. No pleasanter object can be met in a summer-day's ramble than a group of the *mädchen*, with their hair neatly folded, smooth on the brow and plaited behind, with the smart embroidered cloth or velvet head-dress, and the gilt paper-cutter passed through the hair; neat [284] shoes and blue stockings are shown by the sensible length of the petticoats, and a gay handkerchief sets off the firm bust. Their figures are lithe and upright, though somewhat thick and substantial. The paper-cutter in the head is supposed to represent a nail of the Cross.

As housewives, the Germans are doubtless unsurpassed by any other nation; the houses are clean, the stoves shine brightly, and they are for ever washing clothes in the river. We cannot applaud the way in which they cook their meat generally, but their puddings are admirable. At Cochem our landlady used to send us up soufflèd puddings that would have done credit to the Palais Royal. On the Moselle the old-fashioned spinning-wheel is to be seen in every village, and knitting is always taken in hand when walking or superintending household affairs.

Singing is constantly heard in the evening, and many of the little coteries in the townlets by our river's side subscribe to hire a piano from Coblence or Trèves, and by the aid of its music they make lively the long hours of darkness in winter.

The priests seem respected, and on amicable terms with all classes, but generally they do not hold the same social position that they do in this country.

If the traveller on the Moselle is himself not over-exacting, and ready to meet civility half-way, he will find all those he encounters polite and pleasant, and he cannot fail of spending an agreeable time on the banks of our charming river. [285]

The Roman poet Ausonius, who about the year A.D. 370, when passing through the dense forests that covered all Germany, suddenly came out on the Moselle near Neumagen, was so struck with the beauty of the river that he explored its course, and then wrote a poem thereon. The palaces and the buildings he mentions have all passed away, but the natural beauties remain; and the old castles that at the present time adorn the tops of the hills quite make up for the towers that are gone.

Now, as then, the vine grows luxuriantly over the cliffs, the peaceful river flows calmly on; and the people dwelling on its banks are simple, loyal, and brave.

We have now reached and described Coblence, and with Coblence ends the Life of the Moselle. We have sat with her beneath the forest shade that shelters her birthplace in the Vosges mountains; we have day after day wandered by her side as she bounded along in all the freshness of her youth, or as, in later days, she floated on majestic in her beauty; we have slept night after night, lulled by the ripple of her waters; we have climbed among her mountains and her forests; we have mused or sung amidst her ruins; we have dreamt of other days, of olden times, of things that come not again save in such dreams; we have also, it is to be hoped, in some measure, profited by our communion with the great heart of Nature,—something, we trust, we have learnt of that inner life which makes the very stones and earth preach to us of their Divine origin. [286]

By the Moselle we have found flowers growing, beautiful in their forms and colours, but more beautiful in their uncultured wildness; we have listened to the songs of the gay birds as we rested in the woods; the clouds have fleeted through the pure blue vault, rain has freshened earth and sun has ripened her fruits: all these, and many other incidents, have striven to teach us to love and reverence the great heart of Nature; that heart which, if the Painter, with all his skill of colour or of handiwork, fail to express, he sinks back into the mere copyist; if the Poet feel it not or love it not, his bark is stranded on a barren shore; and what would music be without it?

If, then, the Moselle has whispered or suggested to us aught of this heart, this inner life of Nature, let us preserve it within us pure and beautiful, as all things in Nature are; so shall our summer's tour have not been made in vain, nor useless been the life of the Moselle.

Standing at that spot where the Moselle and Rhine are met, we now take leave of our dear river.

Night is in the heavens, the still cold night of winter; the stars look down upon us with their eyes of love; the great fortress of Ehrenbreitstein looms hugely over the Rhine stream, telling of war and horrid strife, but on the shore of the Moselle rises a fair church, telling of peace. The fortress shall crumble and decay, but the church shall, in the end, remain when all else has passed away.[287]

The light of the stars falls coldly on the waters; the air is chill and frosty; if we look further, we perceive in the distance forms of beauty floating on: dark is the night around, but the stars are bright. So with us, all is often dark and dreary; the very light we have, seems cold, but if we search earnestly into Nature's heart, and follow her guidance, she will lead us where those faint shining stars become great worlds of light; and they, the footstools of still higher realms, shall guide us to Heaven itself.

THE END.

[288]

Made in the USA
Monee, IL
27 January 2023

26479406R00056